Socrates
and Athens

David M. Johnson

CAMBRIDGE UNIVERSITY PRESS
Cambridge, New York, Melbourne, Madrid, Cape Town,
Singapore, São Paulo, Delhi, Mexico City

Cambridge University Press
The Edinburgh Building, Cambridge CB2 8RU, UK

www.cambridge.org
Information on this title: www.cambridge.org/9780521757485

First published 2011
Reprinted 2013

Printed in India by Replika Press Pvt. Ltd

A catalogue record for this publication is available from the British Library

ISBN 978-0-521-75748-5 Paperback

Contents

Preface

Socrates is one of the ancient Greeks that everyone's heard of. Most people have even heard of something called 'the Socratic method'. And Socrates' trial in 399 BC is one of the most famous miscarriages of justice in history, right up there with the trials of Jesus of Nazareth (*c.* AD 30) and of Galileo (in AD 1633). Yet Socrates' deepest influence may be more subterranean: whether you know it or not, he's helped shape how you think about yourself and your life. He is responsible, more than any other individual, for adding a new urgency and vigour to the fundamental questions we ask about our own lives. What is the best sort of life? And what kind of person must I become if I am to lead that sort of life?

Given the 2,400 years since Socrates' execution, it is hardly surprising that what most people have heard about Socrates bears only a passing resemblance to what our earliest sources tell us about him. Socrates, it turns out, was always rather mysterious, and intentionally so. He was more interested in making people think than in telling them what to think. This doesn't mean that we can't know anything about him: we can study the sorts of questions he liked to ask, the reasons he asked those questions, and the sorts of answers he found promising. And we can put Socrates and his trial into their original historical context. The goal of this book, then, is to help readers rediscover the original Socrates, or at least several original Socrateses – Socrates as he appears in our earliest sources.

Socrates' trial is naturally one focus of this book. A spate of recent books (see the Further Reading section at the end of this volume) has presented rival interpretations of the trial. But the best way to study the trial is to read the primary sources with enough informed help to make good sense of them. Hence I provide a translation of the full text of Plato's *Apology*, Plato's version of Socrates' defence speech (*apologia* means 'defence speech' in Greek), which is our most important source for the trial, and I discuss the intellectual and political climate behind the trial in this introductory chapter. This isn't, however, just another volume with texts about the trial of Socrates: included here are the bulk of Plato's *Laches*, one of the most characteristic (and easily accessible) of his early dialogues, and some meaty excerpts from the *Euthydemus* and *Gorgias*.

Another special feature of this book is the emphasis on Xenophon (*c.* 430–*c.* 355 BC) as a source for Socrates. One chapter is given over to Xenophon here, and evidence from Xenophon plays an important role in the first chapter. Xenophon was, like his contemporary Plato (429–347 BC), a follower of Socrates, and he wrote a number of works about him. But Xenophon was not a full-time philosopher, and his Socrates is in important ways different from Plato's. Plato's Socrates is far more important from a philosophical point of view, so most modern scholars emphasize Plato and neglect Xenophon. Plato is also the greater literary artist, and my own general characterization of Socrates here will owe more to Plato than Xenophon. But if one of our goals is to study Socrates in his original context, we should not ignore a writer who knew him for almost as long as Plato did, and had access to many written sources about Socrates now lost to us. Too often Xenophon's Socrates is rejected as a less interesting rival of Plato's; I believe that Xenophon did not aim to reject and replace Plato's portrait so much as to correct and supplement it. If this is true we need not choose one author or another, but can productively read both together, as I hope will be the case with this volume.

To a few notes on style. I generally use Latinized versions of Greek names, in keeping with the practice of the authoritative and handy *Oxford Classical Dictionary*. The glossary provided should help you keep track of key figures and terms. Such items are printed in **bold** at their first appearance in each chapter to remind you that they can be found in the glossary. Dates are BC unless otherwise indicated. Macrons (long marks) are included the first time a Greek word appears and are also shown if that word appears in the glossary.

Texts from Plato are cited with Stephanus numbers, a handy method of citing any edition of Plato. These numbers derive from a famous early print version of Plato's Greek text, published in 1578 by Henri Estienne (Stephanus in Latin). Stephanus numbers refer to the pages in this edition, letters (usually a–e) to sections of those pages. These are the numbers you'll see in the margins of selections from Plato. References to Xenophon's major Socratic work, the *Memorabilia*, are by book, chapter, and section numbers: for example, *Memorabilia* 4.2.1 refers to the first section of the second chapter of the fourth book of the *Memorabilia*. Xenophon's other Socratic works are not split into books, so references to them contain only two numbers, chapter and section (*Oeconomicus* and *Symposium*) or only one number, section (*Apology*). When a reference is made to a text quoted in this volume, the numbers are printed in **bold**.

Finally, let me offer my thanks to Eric Dugdale for suggesting this project to me and providing a tremendous amount of helpful feedback along the way. I also thank James Morwood for his feedback and kind words. The remaining errors, to make use of one of Socrates' paradoxes, are certainly not intentional; but they are mine.

1 Introduction: Socratic questions

> Socrates was the first to summon philosophy down from the heavens, to have her take her place in cities and lead her even into our homes, and to compel her to investigate life and character and good and evil.
>
> (Cicero, *Tusculan Disputations* 5.10)

The questions Socrates asks

Most philosophers are remembered mainly for their conclusions. Socrates is remembered above all for his questions, for his way of pursuing philosophy. Hence it is fitting that most people have heard of the Socratic method, even if they can't name a philosophical position Socrates held – and even if, as we shall learn, the phrase 'Socratic method' is often used today in a sense Socrates himself would have rejected (see the text box on pp. 93–4). Socrates' questions matter so much because, as the Roman **Cicero** (106–43) notes in the quotation above, they brought philosophy home. Socrates' greatest student, **Plato** (*c.* 429–347) has a prominent Athenian general remark on the impact of Socratic questioning.

NICIAS   I don't think you understand what must happen whenever anyone comes into close contact with Socrates and gets into a conversation with him. Even if conversation starts off on some other topic, it never ends until Socrates argues him around to having to account not only for the way he lives his life now but for the life he has led before. Once this starts, Socrates will not let him off the hook until he has put everything about him well and truly to the test.

(Plato, *Laches* 187e–188b)

And Socrates wasn't content with just any sort of answer to these probing questions. He wasn't looking to discuss famous exemplary people, heroes of Greek myth or Greek history, nor was he willing to stop once he'd identified individual actions that were particularly admirable. He demanded clear *definitions* of the characteristic traits of a good person, the **virtues**. And he wasn't content with mere dictionary definitions: he wanted definitions that explained what these qualities really are. He was confident that the virtuous person would have a good life, and that the knowledge expressed by accurate definitions was an essential ingredient, and perhaps the only essential ingredient, in virtue.

Socrates never found fully satisfactory answers to his questions. But this lessened neither his commitment to the pursuit of virtue nor his resolve to do what virtue, inasmuch as he understood it, demanded that he do. Thus Socrates' recognition of the limits of human wisdom did not lead him to moral relativism, but was part of his distinctive commitment to morality. There is something particularly appealing about this mixture of intellectual and moral integrity.

But not all people found, or find, Socrates appealing. You may not. Many students, and among them some of the most thoughtful, initially find Socrates more annoying than enlightening. This brings us to the other thing that most people know about Socrates: his trial. He was executed in 399, at the age of 70, by his home city, Athens, the world's first democracy. Much about that trial, as we will learn, is uncertain and controversial. But Plato has Socrates attribute the Athenians' hatred of him to his habit of asking difficult questions (see *Apology* **23a–24b** on pp. 42–6). Socrates had an intensely annoying habit of demanding that prominent people explain themselves, and then making it all too clear that those people did not really know what they thought they knew. Thus the same thing that made Socrates so influential in his own day, and that has kept people talking about him for all the centuries since he died, led him to his death.

Socrates himself wrote nothing – until, perhaps, a poem or two when he was awaiting his execution in jail, as Plato reports at *Phaedo* 61b. We must therefore rely on other sources to learn about him. Before going any farther, then, it will be best to consider each of those sources in turn.

Our sources for Socrates

Aristophanes

Aristophanes (*c.* 455–386) was the leading comic playwright of his day. Socrates is the central figure in Aristophanes' *Clouds*. This play takes its title, like many ancient comedies, from its chorus; in our play the clouds are goddesses worshipped by a Socrates who is unwilling to recognize any of the traditional gods. The play was put on in 423 BC, but placed third in the three-way competition that year. Aristophanes revised the script, and it is this revised script that we have, though Aristophanes never staged this edition.

The protagonist of the play is an elderly Athenian named Strepsiades, who turns to Socrates in hopes of learning how to argue his way out of his debts. Socrates isn't really interested in teaching Strepsiades what Strepsiades wants to learn, and gives up on him after spouting various comic versions of contemporary scientific lore and then failing to teach him ridiculous bits of Greek grammar.

After Strepsiades drops out, his son, Pheidippides, learns rather more in Socrates' school. We see that the school is inhabited by a pair of personified arguments, Right and Wrong, who showcase their debating skills, and their morality and immorality, to allow Pheidippides to choose which he will study under (lines 889–1104). Right stands for good old-fashioned Athenian values, but isn't exactly quick on his feet, and is something of a lecherous old man. Wrong boasts of his ability to teach you how to argue your way out of any fix. And he wins the debate. Pheidippides vanishes into Socrates' school, and when he reappears he has been so well trained that he can prove to his father that it is perfectly fine to beat not only your father but your mother. Strepsiades, outraged, burns down Socrates' school.

By introducing the characters Right and Wrong, Aristophanes distances Socrates from the most subversive arguments in the play. But while Socrates himself does not make such arguments in his own voice, the audience no doubt was meant to associate him with Wrong's arguments. And Aristophanes' Socrates is certainly impious; as we'll see, in *Clouds*, line 367, he brazenly claims that there is no such thing as Zeus (quoted on p. 22). No wonder that the jury at Socrates' trial in 399 remembered the Socrates from the play, and not fondly.

Scholars are divided on whether or not Aristophanes meant the *Clouds* as an attack on Socrates in particular or instead used him as a sort of poster-child for everything Aristophanes found ridiculous or dangerous about contemporary intellectuals. In Plato's *Apology* (**19d**, pp. 34–5), Socrates simply denies that he knows anything at all about the sort of natural philosophy he is associated with in the *Clouds*. But, as we will soon see (pp. 22–3), there are hints elsewhere in our sources that Socrates did indeed have some interest in such matters. And Aristophanes' attack on Socrates may be more subtle than the jokes would lead us to believe. Aristophanes' Socrates is not so much immoral as amoral: he casts doubt on traditional morality but fails to replace it with anything else. Aristophanes was a comic playwright, not an intellectual historian, and so certainly was not overly concerned with portraying Socrates accurately. But for his parody to have the greatest impact, it would have to be directed at Socrates rather than at some artificial composite intellectual.

An ancient anecdote has it that when non-Athenians at the original performance of the *Clouds* were wondering who this Socrates fellow was, Socrates himself stood up and then remained standing throughout the whole play (Aelian, *Varia Historia* 2.13). By standing up Socrates answered the question of the non-Athenians, but by remaining standing he may have raised another question, especially for the Athenians in the audience: am I really the outrageous fool that Aristophanes presents me as?

Plato

Plato (*c.* 429–347) came from a wealthy family that was active in Athenian politics. During his teens and twenties he was one of the young men who associated with Socrates. Around 383 he founded an informal school that was called the Academy, as that was the name of the public gymnasium complex at which Plato and his students met. The Academy would offer varied interpretations of Plato's philosophical legacy for almost 300 years, until the sack of Athens by the Romans in 86.

Plato was still more influential as an author. Almost all of his writings are dialogues featuring historical characters in conversation with Socrates, and many of these conversations are given fairly exact dates and settings. Socrates and his contemporaries come vividly to life in Plato's writing, tempting us to believe that we are overhearing Socrates' very words. But Plato's dialogues are not straightforward evidence for the historical Socrates. Ancient readers would not have expected Plato to give word-for-word accounts of actual conversations: in antiquity, even historians were given leeway to present historical characters giving speeches that were substantially composed or at least revised by the historians themselves. And the philosophy expounded in Plato's dialogues varies widely. Plato's thinking presumably developed over his long career, and it is natural to assume that, over time, his ideas came to diverge more and more from those of Socrates. Thus, at least in some of his later dialogues, Plato puts his own ideas into Socrates' mouth, ideas that would never have occurred to Socrates himself.

If we knew which dialogues Plato wrote when, we'd have a good idea of where to begin our attempt to disentangle Socrates' ideas from those of Plato. But we have no direct evidence for the publication dates of Plato's dialogues, and references to datable external events in the dialogues are relatively rare. We must therefore rely mainly on internal signs in the dialogues themselves, and above all on changes in Plato's style. Scholars have diligently studied Plato's style for well over a hundred years, employing a set of techniques known as '**stylometry**'. Such techniques study the linguistic habits of an author, and how they vary over time. Stylometric analysis allows us to outline the broad development of Plato's style, and to group Plato's works into three periods, naturally enough labelled early, middle, and late. The consensus view is that while at least some of Plato's early works give a fairly accurate picture of Socrates' thought, the middle and late dialogues for the most part reflect Plato's own and rather different philosophy.

Plato's dialogues

The chart opposite groups the works of Plato solely on stylistic criteria; within each group, the dialogues are listed in alphabetical order. When a dialogue's title is preceded by one asterisk, Socrates is present but in a subordinate role; when it is preceded by two asterisks, Socrates is absent. Dialogues whose titles are put in brackets are those that many scholars doubt were written by Plato.

Early dialogues	Major topic(s)
[Alcibiades]	Self-knowledge
Apology	Socrates' defence speech (**entire work in chapter 2**)
Charmides	Moderation (***sōphrosynē***)
[Clitophon]	Socrates' failure to do more than exhort
Cratylus	Etymology
Crito	Whether Socrates should escape from jail
Euthydemus	Sophistic puzzles (**excerpt in chapter 5**)
Euthyphro	Piety
Gorgias	Rhetoric and virtue (**excerpt in chapter 5**)
Hippias Major	Beauty
Ion	Poetry
Laches	Courage (**the majority is found in chapter 3**)
Hippias Minor	The liar versus the truthful man
Lysis	Friendship
Menexenus	An oration for Athenian war dead
Meno	Virtue and knowledge
Phaedo	Socrates' death and the immortality of the **soul**
Protagoras	The unity of virtue; pleasure as the good
Symposium	A dinner party conversation about love
[Theages]	Socrates' divine sign

Middle dialogues	Major topic(s)
* Parmenides	Plato's forms and Parmenides' 'One'
Phaedrus	Rhetoric and love
Republic	Justice and the ideal city
Theaetetus	Knowledge

Late dialogues	Major topic(s)
* Critias	Atlantis
** Laws	A second-best city
Philebus	Pleasure
* Politicus	Defining the true statesman
* Sophist	Dividing sophistry from philosophy
* Timaeus	A divine craftsman's creation of the world

The stylistic evidence, alas, only takes us so far. Plato may have revised works over years, complicating dating based on stylistic criteria. The *Republic* is a major case in point: many believe that the first book of the *Republic* (the equivalent of a modern chapter) was written years before the later books, and should count as an early dialogue, while the remaining nine books were written later. And there are major differences in philosophical content even among the works dated early on stylistic grounds. Scholars have attempted to come up with a more refined dating scheme for the early dialogues by producing a subset of 'transitional dialogues', so-called because they make the transition from more Socratic early dialogues to the middle dialogues in which Plato introduces his own original ideas. But stylometry does not provide firm evidence for sorting the dialogues within these groups, and no one arrangement of these early dialogues has ever commanded a consensus.

Aristotle (384–322), who was a member of Plato's Academy from 367 until Plato's death in 347, provides us with further evidence for isolating the historical elements in Plato's portrayal of Socrates. Aristotle tells us that while Socrates sought definitions of ethical terms, Socrates, unlike Plato, did not develop a full-blown theory of forms (*Metaphysics* 13.4, 1078b29–30). In Plato's theory of forms, universals like justice are said to have a separate existence which transcends their involvement in individual just people or just actions in the physical world. Aristotle thus believed that he could distinguish between the historical Socrates, who sought definitions but not Platonic forms, and the Socrates in Plato's later dialogues, who presents Plato's own philosophy. Today almost all scholars think that Aristotle was right to deny that Socrates developed the theory of forms, but many scholars argue that Aristotle knew nothing about Socrates other than what he read in Plato. If this is true, Aristotle provides no *independent* evidence for Socrates; we can read Plato just as well as he could. But it is at least some comfort that the traditional approach to Plato – that taking him as first reporting Socrates' thought, then developing his own – is in keeping with the way that Plato's greatest student, Aristotle, interpreted his own teacher.

Platonic silence and Socratic irony

There is yet another difficulty with identifying the historical Socrates in Plato. In his dialogues, Plato never says anything in his own voice. Hence Plato never tells us what he thought Socrates believed. And while Socrates is the main character in all of Plato's early dialogues, Socrates does not simply report his beliefs and arguments: he engages in lively conversations with a varied cast of conversation partners (**interlocutors**). Plato's Socrates is sometimes passionately argumentative, but just as often he is playfully ironic, and most of the time he is a questioner rather than a lecturer. We must interpret what he says in its dramatic setting. Hence what one scholar interprets as Plato changing his mind over time another will chalk up to a different dramatic context.

Even when Plato's Socrates makes a statement rather than asking a question he is often ironical. **Socratic irony** takes a multitude of forms. Often he employs mock praise to ridicule pompous interlocutors; sometimes he seems to ironically overstate the extent of his own ignorance. When Socrates speaks ironically, he may mean the opposite of what he is saying, or merely something different from what he is saying, or he may even both mean and not mean what he is saying, just in different senses. Irony is so important that the most influential scholar of Socrates in the second half of the twentieth century, Gregory Vlastos, gave it prominent play in the title of his major work on Socrates, *Socrates: Ironist and Moral Philosopher*. Vlastos himself was confident that he could analyse and understand Socratic irony in a way that allowed him to draw firm conclusions about Socrates' moral philosophy. But many others have been rather less certain.

To top it all off, Plato has Socrates claim that writing itself is nothing serious, but is best considered a form of play, far inferior to direct oral conversation, and best suited to remind people of things they already know (*Phaedrus* 277d). Certainly Plato's works are playful literary masterpieces, and their complex literary form complicates a straightforward philosophical or historical interpretation.

Xenophon

Xenophon (*c.* 430–*c.* 355), like Plato, was an aristocratic Athenian who knew Socrates as a young man. Xenophon left Athens in 401 and was subsequently exiled from Athens, to return only late in his life, if he ever did. He thus missed Socrates' trial and death in 399, and was not present in Athens during the years Plato and others were discussing Socrates there. But Xenophon was not isolated in exile, and clearly read widely in the Socratic literature that was springing up in the first decades of the fourth century. Among many other works, he wrote four on Socrates.

The most substantial of these is his *Memorabilia* (*Recollections*), a lengthy defence of Socrates that aims to show not only that Socrates was innocent of the formal charges against him, but that he was in fact the most useful adviser, teacher, and friend a man could have. Xenophon's *Apology* gives a brief account of Socrates' deliberations before his trial, his speech at the trial, and some remarks he made subsequently. His *Symposium* (*Dinner Party*), which is pretty clearly a response to Plato's work of the same name, culminates in a long speech in which Socrates argues that love between men should remain unconsummated. Xenophon's *Oeconomicus* (*Estate Manager*) begins with a conversation in which Socrates critiques the conventional understanding of wealth, but then turns to Socrates' lengthy conversation with a most conventional Athenian gentleman, who gives him many a practical lesson on how to run a country estate profitably. Scholars are divided on whether this odd work shows Xenophon putting his own conventional ideas into Socrates' mouth, or is Xenophon's subtle attempt to contrast conventional views with Socratic ones.

We possess even less information for the dating of Xenophon's works than we have for those of Plato. But Xenophon's Socratic works were probably written after Plato's early dialogues, and indeed after much of the early Socratic literature. This needn't mean, however, that Xenophon was simply reworking these works and contributing nothing of his own. Rather, Xenophon often 'corrects' his sources, on the basis of his own understanding of Socrates. Hence in his *Symposium* Xenophon more clearly responds to the charge that Socrates sexually corrupted his youthful companions than Plato's Socrates does. And Xenophon's *Apology* makes it clear that Socrates believed that the time had come for him to die, which explains his uncompromising stance in the courtroom. Xenophon is first and foremost a defender of Socrates; he does not examine Socrates' ideas for their philosophical value, but articulates them while defending Socrates. And his Socrates is not so much an inquirer as a mentor. He spends far less energy in pursuit of the definition of key moral terms, and far more time dispensing moral advice.

The so-called Minor Socratics

Xenophon and Plato were not the only people writing works on Socrates in the decades after his death, but the works of the others survive only in fragments. Among the more important of these 'minor Socratics' was **Antisthenes** (*c*. 446– *c*. 365), who argued that virtue was sufficient for the good life, and rejected pleasure. Antisthenes was considered the inspiration behind the philosophical movement known as Cynicism, whose adherents preached that we ought to live austerely and even primitively, in accord with nature. At the other end of the spectrum was **Aristippus** (*c*. 440–?), who argued that pleasure was the end we should aim at; we shall meet him in chapter 4. The wide divergence between these two followers of Socrates reveals something about the open-ended nature of Socrates' philosophy.

The Socratic Question

It is, then, difficult to find the real Socrates in any one of our sources. Aristophanes' Socrates has been taken to be a comic caricature; Plato's Socrates morphs into Plato; and Xenophon's Socrates has been taken to be a front for Xenophon. And while something can be gained from comparing our sources – Xenophon's Socrates, for example, obviously has far more in common with the Socrates of the early dialogues than with the figure from later Plato – the differences between our sources are so great as to lead many to despair of resolving them.

So who was Socrates? Today most scholars have abandoned the effort to answer this question, which has been debated so long that it has gained capital letter status as **The Socratic Question**. They emphasize differences between our sources rather than attempting to get behind these differences to identify the original, historical Socrates. This approach is prudent and productive. Aristophanes' Socrates, Plato's Socratic dialogues, and the Socratic works of Xenophon are all clearly worth studying in their own right.

But this approach is also unfortunate. Socrates matters, as we have seen, in some large part because of the life he led, a life which led him to his fatal encounter with the Athenian legal system. If we cannot study the historical Socrates but can only study him as a fictional character in this or that author, we've lost much of importance. And the decision to give up on the historical Socrates has sometimes been based on the view that we must dismiss our sources as 'fictional' – as if classifying a work as fiction proves that it can contain nothing historical. No one of our sources was dedicated solely to an accurate presentation of the historical Socrates. But, like students of other aspects of ancient history, we don't need to simply choose one source to trust and then follow it blindly. Nor need we despair when our sources disagree. Some disagreements are only apparent. And where disagreements are real and substantial, we can take into account the intentions of each author and make a reasoned attempt to say which is more in keeping with the rest of what we know about Socrates.

Socrates the satyr

Satyr *Socrates type A* *Socrates type B*

From left to right: satyr from a bronze offering jug, c. 325 BC; marble bust, Roman copy of Greek statue probably dating to early 4th century; marble bust, Roman copy of Greek original of the later 4th century.

We are blessed with so many ancient depictions of Socrates that we think we know what he looked like. We may be wrong. In Socrates' day sculptors were not interested in making realistic portraits. Socrates' portrait was based on his supposed resemblance to a **satyr** (or **silenus**), a mythological creature that took the form of a man with the ears and tail of a horse or goat. So the model for ancient images of Socrates was not so much Socrates himself as a mythological creature he was thought to resemble. The comparison to a satyr was hardly flattering; satyrs are most often shown drinking wine and engaged in various sexual escapades in the company of the god of wine, Dionysus.

Plato and Xenophon discussed Socrates' appearance in characteristically different ways. In his *Symposium*, Plato has **Alcibiades** compare Socrates to a musical satyr, Marsyas: Socrates' words, like the music of Marsyas, were capable of moving men. And Socrates resembled little statues of satyrs which could be opened to reveal treasures within (Plato, *Symposium* 215b–d). For Plato's Alcibiades, Socrates remains strange and even otherworldly: he can be compared to no other man, only to a creature of myth, and no one would guess at the inner beauty hidden within his ugly exterior. Xenophon has Socrates argue that his features are beautiful because they are functional: his bulging eyes allow him to see in all directions, and the nostrils of his snub nose allow him to smell in all directions (Xenophon, *Symposium* 5.5–5.6). While Xenophon's Socrates likely made this argument tongue in cheek, the emphasis on practicality is typical of Xenophon. Thus both Xenophon and Plato tried, in very different ways, to come to terms with Socrates' challenge to the Greek ideal of *kalokagathia*, 'beautiful goodness', the notion that external beauty reflects inner beauty. (For more on the assumed correspondence between beauty and moral worth, see the note at *Apology* **20b**, p. 36.)

Type A portraits of Socrates are thought to derive from a statue commissioned by friends of Socrates and made soon after his death; likenesses deriving from this statue show Socrates with decidedly non-ideal features, by classical standards, in which a mature man would certainly not have a snub nose nor have lost his hair. This statue probably was meant to be provocative: just as Socrates himself refused to accept traditional Athenian values, so too his statue defiantly showed a man whose features did not conform to the idealized norm of his day. Later in the fourth century Socrates was no longer a controversial contemporary, but one of the great men of the past, and his features came to more closely resemble those of an idealized elderly citizen. Note how the fuller hair and beard soften his features in the **type B** bust; there are further signs of age as well, marking him as more human than mythological. Thus both types reflect the intentions of artists that go well beyond accurate representation. The Socratic Question applies to images as well as texts.

- If your college, school or town were going to sponsor a statue of Socrates, which of these two types would you prefer, and why?

Socrates and Athens

Socrates and history

Socrates was born in 469 BC. During his childhood Athens developed into what scholars call a 'radical democracy', a direct participatory democracy in which all adult male citizens were allowed and encouraged to participate in government, and even subsidized with pay for serving as jurors and in other official positions.

Slaves, immigrants, and women, as in other Greek cities, had no role in political life, but Athens' government was nonetheless the most democratic known until modern times. At the same time, Athens was also building an empire which came to include most of the islands in the Aegean Sea, and most Greek city-states on the northern and eastern coasts of the Aegean. Athens' rise led to conflict with her great rival, Sparta, the head of an alliance known as the Peloponnesian League. The conflict resulted in the **Peloponnesian War** (431–404), which ended in the defeat of Athens. Athens was stripped of her empire, and her democracy was replaced by an oligarchy – rule by a few men – known as the Thirty. These 30 Athenians, who were initially backed by Sparta, soon enough turned to murdering their opponents and committing other crimes, and thus came to be called the **Thirty Tyrants**. Athenian democrats left the city but within one year had returned in force and driven out the Thirty. They established an amnesty, which spared all but the Thirty and their closest associates for most crimes committed during their rule. Among the leaders of the Thirty, and perhaps their most brutal member, had been **Critias**, an associate of Socrates and a relative of Plato (his mother's cousin). Charmides, Plato's uncle, was also a prominent supporter of the Thirty.

Socrates was deeply involved in the events of these years. He served in the Athenian army, as Athenian citizens were expected to do, on at least three occasions during the Peloponnesian War: at the siege of Potidaea, which lasted from 432 to 430; at the battle of Delion in 424; and at the battle of Amphipolis in 422. By all accounts he served bravely in all three battles (see the text box on p. 83). While he never sought out any prominent role in Athenian politics (see *Apology* **31c**, p. 61), Socrates was willing to serve on the Athenian **Council**. The Council's 500 members, who were chosen by lot, set the agenda for the Athenian **Assembly**, Athens' chief legislative body, and provided the presiding committee which oversaw each meeting of the Assembly. One day in 406 BC, when Socrates happened to be the one member of this presiding committee chosen (again by lot) to chair a meeting of the Assembly, he was entangled in one of the most controversial cases in Athenian history. As the chair of the meeting he attempted, unsuccessfully, to prevent the Assembly from taking an unconstitutional vote to convict a group of defendants without a proper trial (see the text box on pp. 64–5). Later, when the Thirty Tyrants attempted to get Socrates to assist in their illegal execution of Leon of Salamis, Socrates refused to take part, at considerable risk to himself (see *Apology* **32c–d**, p. 63).

Socrates' most famous involvement in Athenian life came in his own trial, of course, which we will study at greater length below and in chapter 2. Here it will suffice to note his final public act: his decision to accept his death sentence at Athens rather than to escape from jail, as both Plato (*Crito*) and Xenophon (*Apology* 22) confirm that he could have done. With his trial complete, Socrates considered it unjust to undermine the authority of the laws of Athens by escaping from prison, though he continued to deny the justice of the verdict itself. An account of his reasoning can be found in Plato's *Crito*.

Timeline

Date	Athenian history	Socrates
469		Birth
460	**Pericles** dominant at Athens	
c. 436	**Anaxagoras** prosecuted for impiety (?)	
432		Siege of Potidaea (until 430)
431	Start of the Peloponnesian War	
430	Birth of Xenophon	Saves Alcibiades
429	Plato born	
424	Date of the conversation depicted in *Laches*	Battle of Delion
423	Aristophanes' *Clouds* produced	
422		Battle of Amphipolis
421	Peace of Nicias between Athens and Sparta	
418	Battle of Mantinea; death of Laches	
415–413	Sicilian expedition; death of Nicias (413)	
406	Battle of Arginusae	Trial of Arginusae generals
404	Defeat of Athens The Thirty in charge at Athens Alcibiades murdered	The Thirty murder Leon of Salamis
403	Democracy restored	
401	Xenophon leaves Athens	
399		Trial and death
c. 383	Plato establishes the Academy	
c. 355	Death of Xenophon	
347	Death of Plato	

Socrates the ideal citizen

Too often only portrait busts survive, a real shame since Greek statues expressed their meaning through the whole figure, not only the head. This statuette shows a fine example of an idealized 'type B' Socrates. He stands with his cloak carefully wrapped about him as any upstanding citizen would, a pose common among the idealized citizens depicted in contemporary grave reliefs. His upper body is firm, and there is at most a hint of a pot belly. Contrast the far coarser Socrates in the illustration on p. 18, which may better reflect the earliest statue of Socrates. In comparison to that image, we have here a made-over Socrates in a business suit, noble rather than provocative.

Marble statuette, 27.5 cm (11 inches) high; second century BC, based on a type B original.

- How would a philosopher be depicted as dressing today, and what would that say about philosophers?

Socrates and democracy

Thus in 399, when Socrates was put on trial, the Athenians were still smarting from the apparently permanent loss of their empire and by the brief loss of their democracy. Socrates, despite his willingness to serve in the Athenian army and to play a role in Athenian democracy, had been critical both of Athenian imperialism and of Athenian democracy. Xenophon reports that **an accuser of Socrates** made this charge against him:

> By Zeus, he made his associates despise the established laws by saying how foolish it was to establish rulers of the city by choosing lots, while no one would use a lottery to select a helmsman or a carpenter or a flute player or anything of that sort, despite the fact that they do far less harm when they make mistakes than do those who make mistakes about the city's business. And such words encouraged the youths to be contemptuous of the established laws and made them violent.

(*Memorabilia* 1.2.9)

---

an accuser of Socrates   this accuser is often taken to be Polycrates, an author of rhetorical showpieces who wrote an *Accusation of Socrates* some years after the trial of Socrates. But there is no good reason to doubt that these charges were in the air in 399.

Most Athenian public officials were chosen by lot. The lottery was part of the basic framework of the democracy at Athens, as the lot was regarded as the most democratic way of choosing public officials: it ensured that all who wished to serve had an equal chance of doing so. An attack on the lot was thus tantamount to an attack on the democratic constitution of Athens.

Plato has Socrates compare the leaders of Athens' glory days in the mid-fifth century to cooks who feasted people on an unhealthy diet that has left them unhealthy and diseased. Socrates is debating with Callicles, a would-be leader of the city who has praised these same men (see chapter 5).

> You are singing the praises of men who gave them [the people of Athens] feasts and met their every desire. And people say that those men made the city great. What they don't realize is that the city is swollen and festering thanks to these men of old. For they filled her with harbours and shipyards and walls and tribute and that sort of nonsense while moderation and justice were lacking. So when this weakness leads to a collapse, they'll blame those who are advising the city at the time, while still praising **Themistocles, Cimon and Pericles**, who are responsible for their misfortunes. And perhaps they will lay hold of you, if you are not careful, and of my friend Alcibiades, when they lose even what they held of old, in addition to what they acquired more recently, despite the fact that you are not really responsible for their misfortunes, but perhaps merely contributors to it.
>
> (Plato, *Gorgias* 519a–b)

Socrates' friend Alcibiades was the most influential, charismatic and scandalous Athenian leader from his arrival on the scene as a young man in the 420s until his death in 404. Alcibiades was the strongest proponent of the Athenian expedition against Sicily in 415, and was made one of the commanders of that expedition, only to be recalled when his enemies charged him with impiety. In 413 the expedition ended in a massive defeat for Athens, though the city would manage to continue fighting against Sparta for nine more years. In the meantime Alcibiades escaped to Sparta, but after various escapades abroad he was welcomed back to Athens and led her to a number of victories before being removed from office for supposed dereliction of duty. He went into exile again, and was killed soon after the end of the war in 404, probably on the orders of the Thirty Tyrants. Alcibiades was thus a tremendously controversial figure, a two-time exile from Athens, but also one of her most gifted leaders. Socrates' friendship with Alcibiades must have been held against him by many.

Themistocles, Cimon and Pericles   Themistocles was Athens' greatest leader during the Persian Wars and was responsible for the victory over Persia at Salamis in 480; Cimon was among the most influential leaders during the next few decades; Pericles was Cimon's rival and subsequently dominated the Athenian political scene from Cimon's exile in 461 until Pericles' own death in 429.

Socrates was thus associated both with the most controversial democratic leader of the time, Alcibiades, and with Critias, the worst of the Thirty Tyrants. Here's how Xenophon articulates this political attack on Socrates:

> Critias and Alcibiades, who did the most harm to the city, were both associates of Socrates. Critias was the most corrupt, most violent, and most murderous of the oligarchs, and Alcibiades was in turn the least self-controlled, most arrogant, and most violent of all those in the democracy.
>
> (Xenophon, *Memorabilia* 1.2.12)

Fifty years after Socrates' trial a speaker in an Athenian court would put it this way:

> You, gentlemen of Athens, put Socrates the sophist to death because he was shown to have educated Critias, one of the Thirty who destroyed the democracy.
>
> (Aeschines, *Against Timarchus* 173)

Socrates at Ephesus

Another ancient Socrates of type B, this one from a private home in Ephesus. It is clearly labelled SOCRATES in Greek to avoid any ambiguity, though the figure would have been recognizable enough. Scholars debate whether the original type B statue of Socrates was seated, as here, or standing, as in the statuette depicted on p. 13. Certainly philosophers were often pictured seated in antiquity, sometimes on rather grand thrones, though Socrates here sits on a humble bench. This Socrates looks off to the side, perhaps to listen to a (now lost) companion. When this image was painted, Ephesus was a rich city under Roman rule and featured a grand library. Some well-to-do Ephesian chose to display his sophistication by decorating a wall with Socrates.

Painting from Ephesus, c. AD 70, copy of an original of c. 180 BC.

- What sort of people are we most likely to find depicted on the walls of contemporary houses?

Socrates and the sophists

When the speaker just quoted, the orator Aeschines (*c.* 397– *c.* 322), called Socrates a **sophist**, he didn't mean it as a compliment. By Aeschines' day the term could apply, as it regularly does now, to a thinker who twists arguments to his own end, with no concern for the truth. This had not been the original meaning of the Greek *sophistēs*. The term originally referred to any sage or expert, but came to be applied to the new group of itinerant intellectuals who appeared in Greek cities during the middle of the fifth century BC to give lectures and short-term courses for a fee. These sophists attracted crowds, money and controversy. Part of the controversy was simply due to the novelty of what they were offering: professionalized higher education. For before their arrival it was thought that after a basic education in reading, writing, music and athletics, the young male aristocrat would learn how to be a leading man in the city by associating with and imitating his elders over a course of years. The sophists offered a short cut, and made cash more important than connections. Established elders naturally resented these new professors who threatened to usurp their traditional role.

The sophists taught about many things, especially topics we would label 'social science': politics, anthropology, geography, history and the like. Central to much of their thought was the distinction between **physis** (nature) and **nomos** (custom). This distinction allowed sophists to make use of the natural world to scrutinize human customs and law; in Greek the same word, *nomos*, covers both law and custom.

Sometimes this scrutiny could produce greater respect for *nomos*, as when the sophist Protagoras argues, in Plato's *Protagoras*, that the norms of justice and moderation were necessary to raise humans above a bestial state of nature (*Protagoras* 320d–328d). But in popular thought the contrast between *nomos* and *physis* was, above all, subversive: it allowed one to claim that human laws were artificial constructs out of touch with the reality of nature. In Aristophanes' *Clouds* (see pp. 2–3 for an outline of the plot), Pheidippides emerges from Socrates' school with the ability to employ this argument to defend beating his own father. Strepsiades has admitted that he beat his son when he was little, but says he did it with the best of intentions.

PHEIDIPPIDES   Tell me:
    isn't it right for me to care for you like that,
    and beat you, if to care for someone is to beat him?
    Why should your body be immune to blows
    while mine is not? I too, surely, was born free.

'If children cry, why think a father shouldn't?'
You claim it's *nomos* that a child should not do the beating.
I reply that old age is a second childhood.
And the old should cry more than the young
as they've less excuse for doing wrong.

STREPSIADES   But nowhere is it *nomos* that a father suffer this!

PHEIDIPPIDES   Wasn't it a man who passed that *nomos*,
just like you and me, and did he not persuade the men of old with words?
Why then can't I pass a new *nomos* from now on
that lets sons beat their fathers in return?
All those blows we suffered before this *nomos* passed
we'll let go, and charge you nothing in return.
But consider the chickens and the other creatures here:
they fight off their fathers. And how do we differ
except that they **don't pass decrees**?

STREPSIADES   What? Since you mimic chickens in every way,
will you eat dung, too, and sleep perched on a bit of wood?

PHEIDIPPIDES   That's not the same at all, sir, nor would Socrates agree.

(*Clouds* Greek lines 1410–32)

Pheidippides' bogus argumentation shows how the norms – the *nomoi* – that govern our lives can be overturned by sophistry. No wonder Socrates got into trouble, if people thought that he taught this sort of thing.

The sophists also taught rhetoric, the art of persuasion. In the Athenian democracy, skill in public speaking was essential. One not only needed to persuade a large audience in order to convince the Athenian Assembly to adopt a law or take some other action; one also needed to be able to speak before a large jury if one was put on trial, as Socrates would be. In the traditional course of things, young men would acquire expertise in public speaking by attending the Assembly and courts, listening to the debates there, and then critiquing them with friends and mentors

---

'If children cry, why think a father shouldn't?'   a delicious adaptation of line 691 of the *Alcestis,* a play by Euripides. The god Apollo has granted Admetus the opportunity to avoid death if he can find someone to die in his place. The decidedly self-absorbed Admetus asks his father to volunteer; he replies, 'You love life, why think that fathers don't?'

it's *nomos*   that is, it's customary or acceptable. But in this passage *nomos* also means 'law', so I've left this word in Greek to make the argument (or joke) clear.

don't pass decrees   for the enlightened Pheidippides, the only significant difference between humans and chickens is that we pass laws while they do not. Strepsiades will note some other pertinent differences, showing that chicken behaviour isn't a good guide for human behaviour. But he's too rattled to realize that he has won the argument in logical terms.

afterwards. The sophists offered a quicker way: pay my fee and I will give you the skills you need to get ahead. Some sophists boldly claimed to be able to argue any side in any case, to 'make the weaker case the stronger', make a losing case a winner, even if this meant making wrong seem right. In Plato's *Apology* (**18c**, p. 32) Socrates says that many were prejudiced against him because they believed that he was the sort who makes the weaker argument appear stronger. They, as Aeschines would do 50 years later, thought Socrates was a sophist.

Socrates learning to love

Bronze relief once applied to a chest; found in Pompeii.

Here we see a Socrates with decidedly less idealized features than those in the type B portraits like that of the statuette in the illustration on p. 13. This bronze piece was once attached to a chest, and was found at Pompeii, the Italian city destroyed by the eruption of Mt Vesuvius in AD 79. The winged central figure here is clearly Eros, the young son of Aphrodite and her helper in love affairs. Some scholars have found the man to be too heavy and 'coarse' to be Socrates, but they were probably guilty of the sort of idealizing that led to Socrates type B. This Socrates, if it is indeed he, leans on his staff, as Athenian citizens were often shown doing in conversation, but his face is almost grotesque, his upper body is flabby, his cloak spills down his shoulder, and he has a decidedly plump belly. If he is Socrates, the woman could well be Diotima, who taught Socrates about the meaning of love, at least according to Plato's *Symposium*. Alternatively, she could be a *hetaira* (high-class prostitute) like **Aspasia**, who was said to have plied that trade before – and during – her relationship with the statesman Pericles, and whom Socrates several times praises, or perhaps Theodote, a glamorous *hetaira* Socrates visits in Xenophon's *Memorabilia* (3.11). The piece is probably meant to be humorous: behold the austere philosopher learning the secrets of love from a woman. The coarseness of Socrates' features adds to the fun. The necklace the woman has taken from the small chest held by Eros perhaps resembles items kept in the chest this bronze piece once decorated. So much for philosophy: jewellery is the real secret to your lover's heart.

Socrates, Greek religion and the divine sign

Socrates was charged under the law against impiety. One of the great debates in the scholarship about Socrates' trial has been whether or not this religious charge was actually a front for underlying political motivations. The religious charges were, as we shall see below, no mere pretext. But neither were they unrelated to the political climate. It is anachronistic to assume that politics and religion could be readily disentangled in Athens. Religion was deeply embedded in all aspects of Athenian life. Tragedies and comedies, for example, were put on at religious festivals, as were athletic competitions. So an ancient Athenian would not have recognized any clear division between religion and politics, and would have had no motivation to question, as modern scholars have, whether Socrates' trial was really about politics or about religion. It was about both.

So why was Socrates considered impious? Xenophon has Socrates wonder what his main accuser, **Meletus**, was up to.

> First of all, gentlemen, I wonder just how Meletus thinks he can say that I don't recognize the gods the city recognizes. For everyone who was there has seen me sacrificing at communal festivals and at the public altars – as could have Meletus, had he so wished.
>
> (Xenophon, *Apology* 11; compare *Memorabilia* 1.1.2 and Plato, *Euthydemus* 302c–303a)

Thus just as our sources provide some evidence that Socrates' service in war and at home showed him to be a loyal Athenian citizen, so too we have some evidence that he did the sorts of things any pious Athenian would do.

Plato and Xenophon agree that there was one thing in particular that caused religious suspicion about Socrates: his claim that a 'divine sign' (*daimonion*) came to him often to dissuade him from doing something. On the day of the preliminary hearing leading up to his trial, Plato says that Socrates met a young man named Euthyphro, with whom he would have a discussion about piety. Euthyphro asks Socrates what his prosecutor is charging him with.

SOCRATES	It's something very strange to hear, my amazing friend. He says that I am a creator of gods, and he's indicted me for creating new gods and not recognizing the old ones – or at least that's what he says.
EUTHYPHRO	I understand, Socrates. It's because you say the divine sign often comes to you. So he's filed this indictment against you for innovating regarding the divine, and is bringing you to trial in order to slander you, as he knows that most people are receptive to this sort of slander.

(Euthyphro Greek lines 3b)

Plato's Socrates, as we shall see, says a bit more about his divine sign in the *Apology*, but he nowhere attempts to explain it or to show that it was in keeping with conventional Athenian religion. Yet surely this sign must have seemed a heretical innovation to many of Socrates' contemporaries.

Xenophon does attempt to explain Socrates' divine sign. The initial part of his defence (Xenophon, *Apology* 12–13, *Memorabilia* 1.1.2–6) isn't terribly convincing; he fudges the distinction between a personal sign that comes to one man alone and the more public workings of conventional forms of divination such as those resulting from observation of birds or atmospheric phenomena or through inspection of the entrails of sacrificial victims. But Xenophon also explains why Socrates' divine sign should be different; it is Socrates' extraordinary piety that wins him special access to the gods (see *Memorabilia* 1.4.18). In conventional religion, too, the gods give signs to those with whom they are well pleased (see Xenophon, *Cyropaedia* 8.7.22); Socrates, being more pious than any other man, got a special sign.

So in Xenophon's account Socrates' divine sign isn't a personal quirk but a natural reward for his piety. Yet it is still rather puzzling. How can Socrates, who is otherwise so committed to rationality, say that he relies on mysterious divine communication? Numerous attempts to square this circle have been offered. The most promising line of attack is to note that Socrates regularly succeeds, at least after the fact, in coming up with a rational explanation for why the sign was right to tell him what it told him. Thus Socrates' sign, as Xenophon understood it, is neither irrational (as modern philosophers worry) nor impious (as many of Socrates' contemporaries believed). It is both rational and religious.

Socrates and the Presocratics

Elsewhere we find further reasons to wonder about Socrates' religious beliefs. Consider Socrates' entrance in the *Clouds*. Socrates is carried onto the stage suspended on the stage crane, the machine often used to allow gods to make their entrances at the end of plays.

STREPSIADES	Socrates! My dear Socrates!
SOCRATES	Why call on me, thou creature of a day?
STREPSIADES	To beg you to tell me what you're doing.
SOCRATES	I walk on air and contemplate the sun.
STREPSIADES	So you look down on the gods from a basket, but can't do it when you're down on earth. That right?
SOCRATES	Never would I have discovered aerial things aright had I not suspended all my judgement and my thought, to mix them with the subtle air that is akin to them. Earthbound, investigating what is high from down below, I'd have discovered nothing. No, for the earth by force draws down to itself all of judgement's juice. The same thing happens to the ginger plant.
STREPSIADES	What do you mean? Does judgement draw the juice into the ginger? Please come down to me, dear Socrates, So you can teach me what I've come to learn.
SOCRATES	And why did you come?
STREPSIADES	I want to learn how to argue. For I'm being plundered and pillaged by interest payments and nasty creditors and I'm facing foreclosure.
SOCRATES	How did you get into debt without noticing it?
STREPSIADES	It's **a horsey ailment** with a big appetite. But teach me **one of your two arguments**, the one that never pays anything back. Whatever you charge, I swear by the gods I'll pay you.
SOCRATES	Just what gods do you have in mind? First off, we don't accept the gods around here.
STREPSIADES	So what do you swear by? Do you accept only iron coins, like they do in Byzantium?
SOCRATES	Do you want to clearly understand divine matters as they really are?
STREPSIADES	Yes, by Zeus, if that's possible.
SOCRATES	And to have verbal intercourse with the Clouds, our divinities?
STREPSIADES	Definitely.

(*Clouds* Greek lines 223–53)

---

a horsey ailment Strepsiades' son, Pheidippides, was spending far too much money on horses.

one of your two arguments Strepsiades alludes to Right and Wrong, Socrates' assistants who dwell in his school and will appear on stage later in the play.

Socrates now performs a mock religious initiation of Strepsiades, preparing him for the entrance of the Clouds, Socrates' divinities. He then contrasts the Clouds with the rest of the Olympian gods.

SOCRATES   They are the only gods; all the rest is pure nonsense.

STREPSIADES   Come now, by Mother Earth, do you think that Olympian Zeus isn't a god?

SOCRATES   Zeus who? Don't talk nonsense. Zeus doesn't exist.

STREPSIADES   What do you mean?
Who does the raining, then? Explain that to me, for starters.

SOCRATES   These Clouds do, of course. Here's the proof for you:
Have you ever seen it raining without any clouds?
Zeus ought to be able to rain on a sunny day when they're out of town.

STREPSIADES   By Apollo, that fits what you were saying just now.
And here I was thinking it was Zeus pissing through a sieve.

(*Clouds* 365–72)

Socrates will go on to explain that thunder and lightning are caused by various sorts of friction, with comic turns in which thunder inevitably becomes cosmic farting, and the explosion of lightning is compared to a bursting sausage.

Meteorology – minus the fart jokes, alas – was one of the fields studied by the so-called **Presocratic** philosophers, who constructed brilliantly imaginative theories with which they attempted to explain nature in rational terms. It was the Presocratics who had placed philosophy up in the heavens, in the terms of the quotation from Cicero this chapter began with. Their speculation about nature laid much of the groundwork for later scientific thought. Some of them were active in Socrates' day (despite being called Pre-socratics). And contemporaries found their ideas controversial. Aristophanes makes it easy to see why, though of course his comedy distorts things. If we don't need Zeus to explain rain, thunder, and lightning, then what do we need Zeus for? Why pray to the gods for rain if there is a scientific explanation for it? Rather as evolution is controversial in some circles today, Presocratic thought was controversial in Socrates' day.

Aristophanes may not be a reliable source for Socrates' views on the natural world. The views Socrates mouths in the *Clouds* can be traced to a variety of Presocratic thinkers, leading many scholars to conclude that Aristophanes' Socrates does not reflect the historical Socrates, but is rather an artificial creation meant to showcase everything that Aristophanes found ridiculous or problematic in the thought of contemporary intellectuals. In the *Apology* (**19c–d**, pp. 34–5), Plato's Socrates claims that he knows nothing about such things and that no one has ever heard him talking about them. Yet both Plato and Xenophon offer some evidence that Socrates was, at least in one point in his career, interested in Presocratic philosophy. In a conversation set on the day of his execution, Plato has Socrates report that he was once greatly impressed with the thought of one Presocratic, Anaxagoras. Anaxagoras may well have been prosecuted for impiety because of his views (see the note at *Apology* **26d** on p. 52). Socrates was excited to hear that Anaxagoras believed that all things were governed by Mind (*nous*), a cosmic force that arranged everything for the best. But when he read Anaxagoras' works, he was gravely disappointed. According to Socrates, Anaxagoras made no use of his cosmic principle and instead explained everything by mechanical causes. Anaxagoras would explain Socrates' presence in jail by reference to Socrates' bones and muscles, rather than by Socrates' decision that it was better for him to stay in prison and face his punishment than to attempt to escape (*Phaedo* 98b–99a).

Xenophon was also well aware of the controversy surrounding Presocratic science, and, like Plato, he took care to distance Socrates from the Presocratics.

> No one ever saw Socrates doing anything impious or unholy, or heard him saying such things. He did not discuss the nature of the universe as most of the others did, investigating how what the sophists call the 'cosmos' came into existence, or what forces established the phenomena of the heavens; no, he showed that those who concerned themselves with such things were fools.
>
> (*Memorabilia* 1.1.11)

Xenophon goes on to say that Socrates mocked the Presocratics for disagreeing with one another, and chided them for attempting to unravel things the gods had left secret. Human beings should investigate human things, the virtues and vices, and politics, and this is what Socrates did.

But as is so often the case, Xenophon's text seems simpler than it actually is. Xenophon does not quite say that Socrates didn't do natural science. He says that he didn't do it *as most of the others did*. Hence it should not come as a complete shock to see his Socrates engaged in rather detailed speculation about the nature of the physical world. Xenophon's Socrates presents us, in fact, with the first known example of the argument from design (*Memorabilia* 1.4 and 4.3). Socrates argues that human beings have been well designed by a beneficent creator: consider, for example, how well our eyes are protected by eyelids which close when we sleep, lashes which protect us from the wind, and the brow which shields them from sweat. Such features show that human beings are 'the designs of a wise and loving craftsman' (*Memorabilia* 1.4.7).

Now some scholars have doubted whether the historical Socrates actually held such views, arguing that Xenophon has lifted them from some Presocratic source or other, or even from popular beliefs. But there is no clear Presocratic source, and Socrates' argument goes well beyond popular ideas. There is no good reason not to credit Socrates with these ideas.

Today the argument from design is most prominently cited by religious conservatives. But, ironically enough, that would not have been the case in Socrates' day – rather the opposite. For the argument from design threatens to remove the gods from active engagement in the world around us. If all has been set up for the best, then direct divine intervention should be unnecessary. But the basic rites and beliefs of Greek religion entailed a far more active role for the gods: sacrifices to the gods were thought to bring divine favour, which could result in the gods intervening on behalf of their followers. And oracles of the gods could reveal mysteries unknown to mankind. Presocratic science – like all natural science – was based on the premise that the universe could be understood by unaided human reason.

Thus Socrates' view of the natural world was unconventional. But Socrates' interest in the natural world differed from that of the Presocratics because Socrates made science ethical: he integrated study of the natural world with his thinking about good and evil, with the result that natural science supported his ethics rather than undermining it. Plato's Socrates wanted to understand why everything was for the best, and Xenophon's Socrates argued that the world was set up to favour human beings, and thus offered proof that the gods were loving masters we should respect and honour. The gods are both the creators of a universe rationally designed to benefit mankind and the ultimate guarantors of a moral order. Thus Socrates brought philosophy home, brought it down to earth – to allude once more to Cicero's famous description of Socrates – not by giving up all interest in the heavens but by showing the moral consequences of our understanding of the heavens. Yet all many Athenians saw was an impious intellectual undermining traditional values.

The legacy of Socrates

In 399 BC the 70-year-old Socrates was convicted of impiety, and sentenced to die. As we saw above, Socrates declined the opportunity to escape from prison, and was determined to accept his punishment, despite his belief that the jury's verdict was unjust. Instead of attempting to escape, Socrates devoted his last days in prison to further philosophical conversations. In the *Phaedo*, Plato gives us an account of Socrates' last conversation. After he argues for the immortality of the soul, and caps his arguments off with a story about the soul's fate in the underworld, Socrates calmly and willingly accepts his fate. He bids his friends to continue his work by caring for themselves – for their souls – by pursuing the sort of inquiry he has devoted his life to. Then he takes the hemlock poison from a sympathetic guard and drains it; death comes slowly, and painlessly, at least in Plato's account. 'Such was the end', Plato's narrator tells us, 'of our comrade, a man, we would say, who was the best of those we have known, and the wisest, and the most just' (*Phaedo* 118a).

But the story of Socrates doesn't end in that jail cell. The *Phaedo* itself reflects Plato's post-Socratic philosophy, particularly his theory of forms and the arguments for the immortality of the soul that are based on that theory. Plato actually tells us that he was too sick to be present for Socrates' last day (*Phaedo* 59b). The *Phaedo* may accurately depict Socrates' last moments (Plato had ready access to many men who were there), but it is more than a historical document. It is, among other things, proof of the vicarious immortality of Socrates, who would live on, in differing forms, not only among men who knew him, like Plato and Xenophon, but through the centuries. Plato and his student Aristotle after him devoted much of their effort to answering the questions Socrates had raised. So would many other ancient philosophers. The Stoics, following the Socratic Antisthenes and his Cynic followers, admired Socrates' commitment to virtue and his ascetic way of life, and their view of the universe as a rationally ordered whole was inspired, at least in part, by the passages in Xenophon we have been discussing. Some ancient sceptics, on the other hand, claimed to find in Socrates a precursor of their own belief that human beings were incapable of grasping the truth. Of the major philosophical schools in antiquity only the Epicureans disavowed Socrates' thought, but Socrates and his followers had also discussed the role of pleasure in the good life, the central concern of the Epicureans, and one of Socrates' followers, Aristippus, argued that pleasure ought to be our goal in life.

Some early Christians, among them the second-century AD Christian apologist Justin Martyr, would defend Socrates as a man who was unfairly persecuted for his advanced religious beliefs much as Christians would be later, though other Christian authors attacked Socrates along with other pagans. But Socrates was a less visible presence in the Christian Middle Ages, when the most influential strand of ancient philosophy was that of the later Platonic dialogues and Aristotle. Socrates was more prominent among Islamic writers during this period, many of whom made him out to be a forerunner of Islamic sages, rather as Justin had made Socrates a proto-Christian. In Jewish authors Socrates played a similar variety of roles; he most often appeared as an otherworldly sage, but sometimes inspired sceptical arguments meant to show the limitations of pagan philosophy.

Socrates re-emerges as a prominent figure in the mainstream of European thought during the Renaissance. He was one of the heroes of the great French essayist Michel de Montaigne (1533–93), who admired Socrates' humility about the limits of human wisdom, his pursuit of self-knowledge, and his character. Socrates would later play a major role in the philosophies of Hegel, Kierkegaard, and Nietzsche. Georg Wilhelm Friedrich Hegel (1770–1831) named Socrates one of his 'world-historical' figures, the avatar of a new individual morality that came into conflict with the traditional collective morality of his community. Socrates' trial was a tragic but necessary stage in the development of thought. Søren Kierkegaard (1813–55) saw Socrates as a master of irony, in Kierkegaard's sense of 'infinite, absolute negativity'. Kierkegaard's Socrates doubts all prior moral norms, but seems to still retain a commitment to morality. In so doing Socrates makes something like a Christian leap of faith, but without the earnest fervour of Kierkegaard's Christianity.

Friedrich Nietzsche (1844–1900) also considered Socrates a pivotal figure in the development of western thought, but argued that Socrates' rationalism was a degenerate rejection of the best aspects of Greek culture, particularly the non-rational, ecstatic Dionysian strand in Greek thought (named for Dionysus, the Greek god of wine). Early Greek tragedy combined this Dionysian element with a more lucid and orderly Apollonian strand (named for the Greek god of prophecy); but under the influence of Socrates' relentless rationality, the Greeks – and hence all subsequent western thought – abandoned this fertile synthesis for a lifeless, negative rejection of life.

It is difficult not to imagine a wry smile on Socrates' face, had he known of the centuries of discussion and controversy he would inspire. He has been as provocative after his life as he was during it.

Socrates takes the hemlock

Socrates at the Moment of Grasping the Hemlock, *1787, by Jacques-Louis David.*

David's painting is probably the most famous image of Socrates, and it brilliantly illustrates the idealizing of Socrates that began with the 'type B' Socratic tradition. The painting is loosely based on Plato's *Phaedo*. Socrates is here amazingly well preserved for his 70 years, and his muscular chest and noble features contain little trace of the satyr typology of ancient portraits. Socrates' left hand points upward, as does Plato's right hand in Raphael's famous *School of Athens* (illustrated on p. 136); in both cases the gesture emphasizes Platonic metaphysics, in which eternal ideals found in the heavens are what truly matters. With his right hand Socrates serenely reaches for the cup of poison hemlock that will kill him. Much as he has just been released from the shackles that now lie beneath him, so too death will soon liberate him from earthly injustice. Plato put more than 15 people in Socrates' jail cell; David chose to present us with 12, thus reminding us of Christ and his disciples, and Socrates' pointing left arm also recalls that of Christ in Michelangelo's *Last Judgement* on the wall of the Sistine Chapel. Christ was only one of the martyrs David would have had in mind; contemporaries took his painting to refer to those unjustly imprisoned by the French monarchy, which would soon be overthrown by the French revolution.

In addition to the emotionally distraught companions of Socrates and the handsome young guard who cannot bear to look upon the poison he hands Socrates, we see Socrates' family being led off in the background, his wife holding her hand up in a mute farewell. At the foot of the bed, detached from the scene and deep in thought, his pen and parchment laid aside, we see Plato as he would have appeared decades after the death of Socrates, contemplating Socrates' death in his mind's eye. Plato has a character in the *Phaedo* (59b) report that 'Plato, I think, was sick' and so not present for Socrates' death. Sick with grief, perhaps, more distraught even than the disciples of Socrates pictured above? Thus Plato's account of Socrates' death was second-hand at best, and perhaps largely a product of his imagination; so too in David's painting the whole scene takes place in the mind of the elderly figure sitting, his eyes shut, at the foot of Socrates' deathbed.

- **Do such departures from the historical truth take away from the power of David's presentation of Socrates – or Plato's presentation of Socrates? Or can they add to it?**

2 Plato's *Apology*

An open-air courtroom, in Athens, 399 BC. Socrates' accusers, **Meletus, Anytus**, and Lycon, have made their speeches, now lost, accusing him of impiety (for more on the prosecutors see **23e–24a** on p. 44). Socrates now rises to speak in response.

Introduction (*Apology* 17a–18a)

17a **Gentlemen of Athens**, I don't know what effect my accusers' speech has had on you. They almost made me forget who I am – that's how persuasive they were. Yet almost nothing they've said is true. Of their many lies here's the one that amazes me most: they kept saying that you must be careful not to let me deceive

17b you, since I'm a **terribly clever speaker**. Their being shameless enough to say this is the most shameful thing of all, since I'll disprove this as soon as I start speaking and show that I'm no clever speaker at all – unless, that is, they actually call someone who speaks the truth a clever speaker. If that's what they're saying, I'd agree that I'm a public speaker quite unlike them.

Now, as I noted, they've said little or nothing that is true, while from me all you

---

Gentlemen of Athens 'Gentlemen' here shouldn't be taken to imply the jurors are upper class. This translation is inspired by the English 'Gentlemen of the jury'; the Greek says simply 'men of Athens' (which sounds too abrupt in English). The jury for Socrates' trial was made up of 500 male Athenian citizens chosen by lottery from the annual jury pool of 6,000. These 6,000 had themselves been chosen by lot from all male Athenian citizens over the age of 30 who wished to serve in this capacity. Such large juries ensured that defendants were judged by a representative group of their peers, and their large number, together with the double lottery used to choose them, made it hard to bribe a jury. Jurors were paid for their service, though only about half of what a skilled worker could make in a day.

Athens had no legal professionals, no judges or defence or prosecution lawyers. Thus jurors did not only decide the facts of the case, but were left to interpret the relevant laws for themselves, and, where the law did not specify a punishment, to decide on that as well (see the text box on p. 70 for the juror's oath). Defendants had to give their own speeches (though wealthy defendants could pay someone to write a speech on their behalf), and the prosecutors were private citizens motivated by civic duty, hatred for the defendant, or both. All this was in keeping with the Athenian democratic ideal: the people, rather than some group of elite experts, ought to rule.

terribly clever speaker Socrates means that his accusers are claiming that he is a **sophist**, or at least uses sophistic tricks. On the sophists, see pp. 16–18.

17c will hear is the whole truth. But by **Zeus**, gentlemen of Athens, it won't be in beautified language like theirs, adorned with fancy words and phrases. No, you'll hear me say things just as they occur to me, in whatever terms I happen upon, since I'm confident of the justice of what I'm saying. And let none of you expect anything else; for surely, gentlemen, it would not be fitting for a man of my age to come before you and play games with words like some **youngster**.

And here's something, gentlemen of Athens, that I must really ask of you. When you hear me defend myself by **talking just as I normally do** near **the bankers' tables in the Agora** and elsewhere, where many of you have heard me, don't be

17d surprised and **interrupt** me because of this. For here's how it is: this is the first time that I've appeared in court in my 70 years. The language in use here is utterly foreign to me. If I actually were from **out of town**, you'd surely be understanding

18a if I spoke in my native dialect and manner, so what I'm asking now is, as it seems to me, only just. Disregard *how* I speak – perhaps it is better, perhaps worse – and instead give all your attention to this: whether *what* I say is right or not. For this is the **virtue** of a juror, while that of the public speaker is to speak the truth.

Zeus was the chief of the Greek gods; speakers often swear by Zeus to show they are in earnest, but the oath is not particularly strong or religious.

youngster Socrates contrasts his own simple style with the style expected from a young student fresh from studying rhetoric with someone like **Gorgias** (*c.* 485–380), who specialized in highly artificial language that sounded more like poetry than prose. Gorgias often seems to have cared more about what his words sounded like than what they meant, while Socrates claims to care only about the substance of what he is saying. Later Greek stylists would call Gorgias' style 'juvenile'. Meletus, who filed the official indictment against Socrates, is a young man (**25d**, p. 49) who prosecutes Socrates on behalf of the poets (**23e**, p. 44).

talking just as I normally do his habit of questioning and refuting people who claim to know something: see **27a–b** on p. 53.

the bankers' tables in the Agora were used by money-changers and bankers, and located, probably, in the north-west corner of the **Agora**, the commercial and civic centre of Athens. See the map on the next page.

interrupt jurors were not required to sit back passively, and could shout out in protest if they didn't like what a speaker was saying. Socrates repeatedly reminds the jury not to interrupt, presumably when he has said something particularly provocative: see **20e** (p. 38), **21a** (p. 39), **27b** (p. 53), and **30c** (p. 60).

out of town a Greek from outside Athens would speak a different dialect of Greek. Before 404, when Athens lost her empire, citizens of cities subject to Athens had been required to appear in Athenian courts for major cases and any cases involving an Athenian citizen. Athenians were therefore used to hearing foreign accents in their law-courts.

virtue (Greek *aretē*) is a quality that makes a thing or person an excellent example of its kind by enabling it to perform its proper function. The **virtues** of a knife, for example, include having a sturdy handle and a sharp blade.

---

1 Why might Socrates want to distinguish his own manner of speaking from that of his opponents?

2 Is Socrates a 'terribly clever speaker'?

3 Would you, as a juror, be willing to let Socrates speak as he pleases instead of speaking as people normally do in court? If you were on trial for your life, would you ask the jury to make this kind of allowance for you?

4 Can you think of public figures today who make a virtue out of using everyday language in their speeches?

Socrates in the Agora

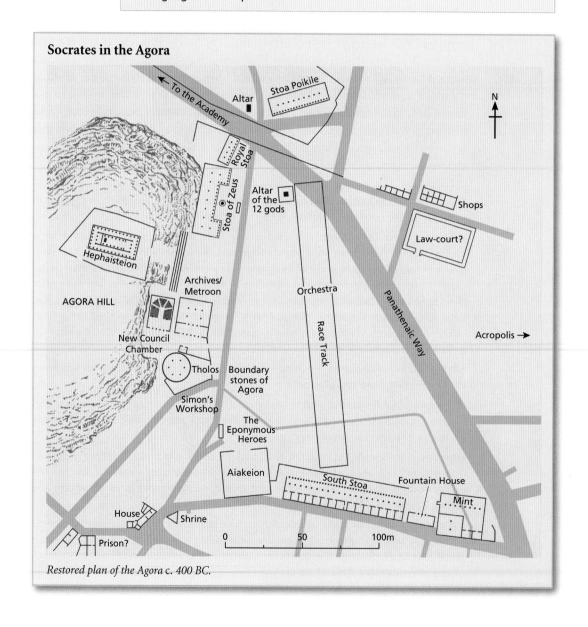

Restored plan of the Agora c. 400 BC.

Socrates, like many Athenians, spent a good deal of time in and around the Agora, the civic centre of Athens. Socrates tells the jury he can often be found talking near 'the tables', apparently somewhere in the north-west corner of the Agora where one could change money (*Apology* **17c**, p. 29). The **Thirty Tyrants** made the Tholos (the round building on the west side) their headquarters, and summoned Socrates there to order him to help kill Leon of Salamis (*Apology* **32c**, p. 63). Under the democracy, the Tholos served as the dining room for the presiding committee of the **Council**. Lectures on **Anaxagoras** could occasionally be heard in the 'orchestra' (*Apology* **26e**, p. 52) in the centre of the Agora. Buildings known as stoas were located around the edge of the Agora, as around many open public spaces in ancient Greece; a stoa combines a covered walkway (or colonnade) with a set of rooms behind it. The covered walkway provided shade in summer and protection from the weather in winter.

The preliminary hearing before Socrates' trial was held in the Royal Stoa to the north-west (*Apology* **19b**, p. 34; cf. **Plato**, *Euthyphro* 2a); this stoa was 'royal' because the Athenian official who had inherited some functions of the one-time kings of Athens did his business there. The Stoa Poikile ('Painted Stoa') to the north would later be the favourite place for lectures by Zeno of Citium, whose followers would be called Stoics after their favoured spot. Socrates' trial may have been held in the building pretty securely identified as a law-court in the north-eastern part of the Agora, but as Athens had many such courts, most not securely identified, we cannot be sure.

Off the south-western corner of the Agora, we have even found what might well be the shop of the cobbler Simon, who is said to have written up versions of conversations Socrates held in his shop (see the illustration on p. 45). The building labelled 'Prison?' was once identified as the prison that held Socrates, but is at least as likely to be a workshop. Archaeologists are often tempted to associate scanty remains of ancient buildings with famous people like Socrates; compare how George Washington is said to have slept in every house on the east coast of the USA built before 1800. What matters most is not that we accurately identify this or that stone as one Socrates stepped on, but rather that we keep in mind that Socrates is not a philosophical abstraction or mere character in a book, but was a man of flesh and blood who lived a real life, one spent largely out in the open, like those of most male citizens of ancient Athens.

The old and new accusations (18a–19a)

The right thing for me to do, gentlemen of Athens, is to defend myself first against the first false accusations against me, against those who were the first to accuse me, and then against the later accusations and accusers. For many have presented you

18b with accusations against me, and for many years now – all of them false. I fear these first accusers more than those with **Anytus**, though they too are dangerous. But the others are more dangerous, gentlemen, since they got hold of you when you were boys and went about persuading you and making accusations no more true than the present accusations are. They said that there was a certain Socrates, a wise man, and a thinker about the **things up above**, who has investigated all **the**

18c **things beneath the earth** and who **makes the weaker argument the stronger**.

Anytus (c. 443–?) was the most influential of the three men prosecuting Socrates, although it was Meletus who officially brought the charges and whom Socrates will question later in the speech (**24d–28a**, pp. 47–54). Anytus was among the leaders of the restored democracy after 403 BC; at **23e** (p. 44) Socrates will say that Anytus was angry with him on behalf of the craftsmen and politicians. Anytus also appears in Plato's *Meno*, where Socrates praises Anytus' father, implicitly criticizing Anytus by contrast. Anytus is also said there to have hated sophists (*Meno* 91c, 92e), and when Socrates argues that leading Athenian statesmen have failed to educate their sons, Anytus warns Socrates not to attack others, lest he be attacked himself (*Meno* 94e). **Xenophon** provides a sort of revenge for Socrates at the end of his *Apology* (29–31), where he says that Socrates predicted that Anytus' son would turn out badly because of Anytus' failure to educate him. The boy, Xenophon reports, did in fact turn out to be a useless drunk. But a later story (Diogenes Laertius 2.43) that Anytus was exiled from Athens soon after Socrates' trial is false: other evidence shows that Anytus was still active in Athens in 396.

things up above here include both atmospheric phenomena (like rain and lightning) and astronomical objects (the sun and stars). The **Presocratic** investigations of these things were controversial because the gods were thought to control such things, and the sun and moon were thought to be divinities themselves; see chapter 1, pp. 20–4.

the things beneath the earth would include matters studied by geologists today, and were also among the subjects studied by the Presocratics. These things were also thought to be controlled by the gods: Poseidon controlled earthquakes, and the underworld and its divinities were located beneath (or within) the earth. In the *Clouds* (187–94), Socrates' students study the underworld by staring at the ground with their backsides comically pointed to the sky, enabling them to do geology and astronomy at once.

makes the weaker argument the stronger one does this by using clever arguments or verbal artistry to make wrong seem right, or at least to make a less justified position appear more justified. Sophists were thought to teach such tricks, and so was Socrates. Socrates' earliest accusers thus lumped him in together with both prominent groups of intellectuals at Athens in Socrates' day, the sophists and the Presocratics. While there was some overlap between the two groups (some sophists popularized Presocratic natural science, among their other interests), the charges against Socrates were certainly painted in pretty broad strokes.

It's these mudslingers, gentlemen of Athens, the ones who gave me this reputation, who are the dangerous ones. For when people hear that someone investigates these things, they think that he doesn't **recognize the gods**. And there are many such accusers, who have been making these accusations over a long period of time now. They spoke to you when you were at the age when you were most prone to believe them, while some of you were still boys or youths, and they really won by default, as there was no one there to defend me.

18d   But the most unreasonable thing of all is that it's impossible to know who they were and report them, unless one of them is a **comic poet**. As for all those who envied me and used slander to persuade you, and also those who were themselves persuaded by these men and persuaded others in turn – it's quite impossible to deal with all of them. I can't bring them back here to examine them; I've simply got to defend myself by sparring with shadows and to conduct my cross-examination with no one here to answer me.

So, as I've been saying, you should recognize that there are two sets of men
18e   accusing me, those who accused me just now and those older ones I've been talking about. And you should recognize that I must defend myself against the old accusers first, for you heard their accusations first, and have heard far more from them than from the later accusers here today.

Well, I must make my defence, gentlemen of Athens, and attempt, in **this short**
19a   **time**, to remove the prejudice you've had such a long time to acquire. I'd like things to turn out this way – if it is better both for you and for me that I have some success in making my defence. But I'm all too aware of how tough this is going to be. Let it turn out as pleases **the god**; the law must be obeyed, and I must make my defence.

---

recognize the gods   the phrase (Greek *theous nomizein*) can refer either to belief in the existence of the gods (which is how Socrates interprets it at **26c**), or to performing the customary rituals concerning the gods.

comic poet   the most influential of the comic poets to attack Socrates was **Aristophanes**, author of the *Clouds*. Aristophanes' contemporaries Eupolis and Ameipsias also ridiculed Socrates in their plays.

this short time   Athenian trials lasted no more than a day, and speakers had to keep to time limits measured by a water-clock. Compare **37a–b** (p. 73).

the god   Greeks often spoke vaguely of 'the god' when they had no particular god in mind, were not sure which god was involved, or did not wish to identify the god involved. There is no commitment to monotheism in this use of the singular. Socrates may possibly be referring here to the god who sends his divine sign (see **31c–d**, pp. 61–2, and **40a–c**, p. 78), but this could hardly have been clear to most of the jury at this point.

1 What are the most important parts of the 'old accusations' against Socrates?

2 Would prior evidence (such as the prejudices that Socrates mentions here) be admissible in a court today? Should it be?

3 Socrates blames comic poets, among others, for his bad reputation. Do comedies (for example, satiric shows on TV) play a similar role today?

4 Does the case of Socrates show why it is important to screen jurors for bias? Would you prefer to be tried by a small screened jury, or by a larger jury more representative of all your fellow citizens?

5 What scientific topics are controversial today? Do we assume scientists aren't religious?

Defence against the first accusers (19a–20c)

19b So let us first examine the accusation which is the source of the slander against me, the slander which Meletus relied on when he brought this indictment against me. Well, just what did they say to slander me? This should be read out just like a sworn statement at a **preliminary hearing**:

> Socrates is guilty and a meddler because he investigates the things beneath
19c > the earth and in the heavens, makes the weaker argument the stronger, and
> teaches others these same things.

That's how it goes. You saw it yourselves in a comedy of Aristophanes, where a certain Socrates **was carried around and claimed that he walked on air** and spouted lots of other nonsense concerning things I don't know the slightest thing about. I don't speak out of disrespect for this sort of knowledge, if there is someone knowledgeable about such things – **may I never face this sort of charge**
19d **from Meletus!** It's just that, gentlemen of Athens, I have nothing to do with these

---

preliminary hearing a preliminary hearing was held before trials; while we don't understand exactly what happened at such hearings – both sides may have had to reveal their evidence – we do know that the prosecutor had to swear an oath confirming his charges, and the defendant had either to admit his guilt or swear an oath that he was innocent. Socrates' preliminary hearing took place at the Royal Stoa in the Athenian Agora: see the map on p. 30.

was carried around and claimed that he walked on air see *Clouds* **225**, quoted on p. 21.

may I never face this sort of charge from Meletus! Socrates makes this wry comment tongue in cheek. Since Meletus hates Presocratic science, he would be prone to attack Presocratic scientists for much the same reasons he is attacking Socrates. There's no way, then, that he would attack Socrates for being *disrespectful* of the Presocratics. Here Socrates is probably showing his own disrespect for Presocratic science, implying that his respect for it is no more real than his fear of Meletus defending the scientists Meletus despises. Both Socrates and Meletus disrespect the Presocratics, but for different reasons; Meletus fears that they will lead people to question traditional morality, while Socrates believes that their claims to knowledge are false.

things. You yourselves I call as my witnesses, the majority of you – all who have heard me talking (as many of you have). Tell the others, then, if you've ever heard me say anything great or small about such things. This way you'll realize that the rest of what most people say about me is also false.

19e   No, none of these things is true, and if you've heard from someone that I endeavour to teach people and **make money**, that's not true either. Though this too seems a fine thing to me, if someone really were able to educate people, like **Gorgias of Leontini and Prodicus of Ceos and Hippias of Elis**. Each of them, gentlemen, can go into any city and persuade the young – who can
20a   associate with any of their fellow citizens they'd like to free of charge – to stop spending time with their fellow citizens, and instead pay money to spend time with them, and feel indebted to them to boot.

In fact, I've heard that there's another man who's come to live here in town, a wise fellow from Paros. I happened to be visiting the man who has spent more money on the sophists than everyone else combined, **Callias**, son of Hipponicus. Now I asked him, since he has a pair of sons, 'Callias,' I said to him, 'if your two sons had been born foals or calves, we'd be able to get hold of a trainer and

---

make money   Plato and Xenophon try to draw a firm line between Socrates and the sophists by emphasizing that Socrates was not paid; Socrates says that those who take money for teaching prostitute themselves (Xenophon, *Memorabilia* 1.6.13). Socrates can, however, honourably accept gifts from his friends, including the 20 *minas* they offer to pay as his fine (**38b** p. 74).

Gorgias of Leontini and Prodicus of Ceos and Hippias of Elis   were famous sophists. Gorgias was introduced in the note at **17c** on p. 29. **Prodicus**, a contemporary of Socrates from the Aegean island of Ceos, was best known for his efforts to distinguish the exact meanings of near synonyms. Hippias, another contemporary of Socrates, came from the Greek city of Elis in South Italy and was an intellectual jack of all trades; Socrates refutes him in Plato's *Hippias Major* and *Hippias Minor*.

Callias   inherited great wealth and a great family name. He lost much of his wealth, in part through extravagant spending, and led a scandalous personal life. We are told (by Andocides, in his speech *On the Mysteries*) that Callias fathered a child with his mother-in-law, Chrysilla. Callias' affair with Chrysilla led his wife (Chrysilla's daughter, of course) to attempt suicide and flee the house. Callias then drove out Chrysilla as well. Callias had inherited the priestly duty of officiating at a religious ceremony at which Athenian children from his clan were registered as citizens, and when Chrysilla's child was brought before him he denied that he was the father. But he was eventually shamed into acknowledging his son and marrying Chrysilla. That child is one of the pair of sons discussed here.

20b   pay him to make them **admirable and good** in the appropriate virtue. He'd be a horse-trainer or farmer. But since your sons are human beings instead, whom do you plan to put in charge of them? Who is knowledgeable about this sort of virtue – the virtue of a human being and citizen? No doubt you've looked into this, since you have sons. Is there such a person,' I said, 'or not?'

'Absolutely,' he said.

'Who?' I said. 'And where is he from and what does he charge to teach?'

'He's **Evenus of Paros**, Socrates,' he said, 'and he charges **five minas**.'

20c   And I deemed Evenus blessed if he really had this **skill** and taught at so moderate a price. I myself would preen and put on airs **were I to know such things**. But I do not, gentlemen of Athens.

---

admirable and good   renders a difficult to translate Greek phrase, *kalos kai agathos*; the first term, *kalos*, means both 'beautiful' and 'admirable', the assumption perhaps being that outward beauty reflects inner worth, or at least that there is an inner worth every bit as worthy of being called 'beautiful' as visible beauty. In Xenophon's *Oeconomicus* (6.12–17), Socrates begins his search for a man who is truly 'admirable and good' with handsome men, and is, unsurprisingly, quickly disappointed. He turns instead to the wealthy and respectable Ischomachus. As the example of Ischomachus shows, the phrase had a certain aristocratic flavour, and in some contexts is well rendered by 'gentleman'. Here Socrates rather comically applies this concept to horses and cows. For virtue see the note at **18a** on p. 29.

Evenus of Paros   was a contemporary of Socrates, and a poet as well as a teacher of rhetoric.

five minas   was a substantial sum, but far less than the 100 minas Protagoras and Zeno are said to have charged for their courses. There are 100 drachmas in one mina, and a drachma was a daily wage in Socrates' day. In Xenophon's *Oeconomicus* (2.3), we are told that all of Socrates' property, including his house, was worth about five minas. To qualify as rich at Athens, one needed a net worth of something like 180 minas. Poor Socrates was far from that and would have had to give up everything he owned to take Evenus' five-mina course. For more on Socrates' wealth, see the note at **23c** on p. 43.

skill   translates the Greek *technē*, which is often translated as 'art', but is not restricted to the fine arts. If you understand what you're doing, and can explain your actions and your subject-matter to others, you possess a *techne*.

were I to know such things   Socrates consistently denies that he is able to teach anyone anything, or at least that he is able to teach them how to be virtuous. But there is some sense in which his denial is ironic, as he says later that he does the people of Athens a great service by calling upon them to concern themselves with the improvement of their souls (see **29d–30b** on pp. 57–8). Socrates cannot make people fully virtuous (as the sophists apparently claim to do), but he can, it seems, make them *more* virtuous.

1 What is Socrates' proof that he doesn't do science or practise sophistry?

2 Does Socrates think Presocratics or sophists really possess valuable knowledge?

3 Why do you think the Athenians were suspicious of professional teachers from out of town?

4 Discussing educating the young with Callias is a bit like discussing it with the latest celebrity to have been mired in some sex scandal (see the note at **20c**, p. 35 for Callias' scandalous life). Why do you think Socrates brings up Callias at all, then?

5 Who are the modern-day sophists, the people who'll teach you how to succeed, for a fee? Self-help gurus? Management consultants? Financial advisers? Teachers?

Socrates and the wise men

Mosaic from Apamea, AD 350.

Socrates has here been promoted to become the head of the Seven Wise Men of ancient Greece, though only two of the six bearded elders surrounding him fit into our photo. The Seven Wise Men, a collection of sages and statesmen from various parts of Greece, lived well before the time of Socrates. This image of Socrates is still just recognizable in terms of earlier and perhaps more accurate images (note his baldness), but here Socrates is far more a timeless champion of eternal pagan philosophical values than a historical figure from a particular point in time. By the time this mosaic was produced, the image of a learned teacher surrounded on both sides by lesser figures had been adopted for Jesus and his disciples (most familiar today in the form of Leonardo's *Last Supper*). This mosaic probably came from a school for Neoplatonic philosophy, a late version of Platonism that provided a rival to Christianity. Members of the school could thus draw inspiration from Socrates, a patron saint of pagan philosophy, and imagine themselves as sages in his company.

Socrates and the Delphic oracle (20c–24b)

Well, **perhaps one of you might object**: 'But, Socrates, what's up with you? Where has this slander come from? Surely you can't have developed such a reputation and provoked talk like this if you haven't done anything out of the ordinary – you must have been doing something different from what most people do. Tell us what it is,

20d so we're not left grasping at straws.'

Anyone saying this would have every right to do so, it seems to me, and I'll try to show you just what has led people to call me wise and slander me. Do hear me out. Perhaps some of you will think that I'm joking, but you can be sure of this: I will tell you the whole truth.

Gentlemen of Athens, I got this reputation through nothing else than wisdom of a sort. What sort of wisdom? It's *human* wisdom, perhaps, for in this sense I just may

20e be wise. And perhaps those men I was talking about just now have superhuman wisdom – if they don't, I don't know what to say about them. I for my part do not have such knowledge, and anyone who says I do is lying and speaking to slander me.

And please don't interrupt, gentlemen of Athens, not even if you think that I am boasting. For **the tale I tell is not my own**; instead, I'll provide you with a source you'll find trustworthy. As witness to my wisdom, if that's what it is, I'll provide the

21a **god at Delphi**. I bet some of you knew Chaerephon. He was a friend of mine from

---

perhaps one of you might object   a speaker in an Athenian court had only one speech to give, and so had good reason to raise and refute hypothetical objections. In the *Apology*, Socrates takes this to an extreme, producing a great array of speeches within speeches. Even in dialogue Socrates is fond of producing imaginary give and take of the 'if I said this, then one would say that' variety (as for example at *Laches* **193e** on p. 91). This allows him to maintain an informal and engaging conversational tone while still retaining control of the conversation.

the tale I tell is not my own   an allusion to a famous line in Euripides' lost play, *Melanippe the Wise*. Melanippe cites her mother as she introduces an account of the origins of the world that owes much to the Presocratic Anaxagoras.

god at Delphi   Apollo's oracle at **Delphi** in central Greece was the most important oracle in the Greek world (see the illustration on p. 112). There were two ways of consulting the oracle. In the more elaborate (and expensive) version, the Pythia, a local woman who served as Apollo's priestess for life, would enter a sort of trance and respond with words, often rather obscure, in response to the question asked of her. These would then have been translated into poetry by male interpreters – poetry which was often still ambiguous. In a simpler rite, a black or white bean would be drawn, giving only a yes or no answer; this is presumably the method Chaerephon used. Cities and individuals consulted the oracle, most often about religious matters, but also to get advice about a wide range of actions, and sometimes, as in the case of Socrates, to determine who was most expert in a given area. For Xenophon's rather different account of the oracle about Socrates, see pp. 112–13.

a young age, as well as being a friend to most of you, a man who shared **your exile and returned with you**. You know what Chaerephon was like, how enthusiastic he was about everything he did. Once he went to Delphi and was bold enough to ask the oracle this question – and as I've said, don't interrupt, gentlemen – he asked if there was anyone wiser than I am. The Pythia replied that no one was wiser. Chaerephon's brother here will testify to this, since Chaerephon himself is dead.

21b   Here's why I'm telling you this: I'm going to explain to you where the slander against me came from. When I heard what the oracle said I thought it over like this. 'Just what is the god saying? And just what does his **riddle** mean? For **I don't know of anything great or small that I am wise about**. So just what does the god mean by saying that I am the wisest? Surely he can't be lying, as that wouldn't be right for him.'

For a long time I had no idea what he was saying. Then, with great reluctance, I resorted to the following way of investigating this. I went to one of those thought

21c   to be wise. For here, if anywhere, I would be able to refute what the oracle said and tell it, 'This man here is wiser than I, but you said I was wiser.' So I examined this man – I don't need to give his name, but it was while I was investigating one of the

---

your exile and returned with you Chaerephon was thus a loyal democrat who joined the democratic resistance in exile during the rule of the Thirty Tyrants in 404–403, and returned to Athens with the democrats who defeated the Thirty. Socrates implies that the majority of the jury were also loyal democrats who had gone into exile; for them Chaerephon would be not only a reliable witness but perhaps also a democratic character witness for Socrates, who had stayed behind in Athens rather than going into exile with the democrats. For Socrates' run-in with the Thirty, see **32c–d**, p.63.

riddle the responses of the Delphic oracle were often obscure or ambiguous. The Lydian king Croesus was famously told that if he attacked Persia he would destroy a great kingdom; attacking confidently, he was defeated and lost his own kingdom (Herodotus 1.53). When Croesus complained afterwards, the god replied that he should have asked which kingdom was meant (Herodotus 1.91). Thus some questioning of the meaning of oracles was considered prudent and pious, and Socrates' doubts about the apparent meaning of the oracle are not necessarily impious.

I don't know of anything great or small that I am wise about Socrates' blanket denial of any wisdom whatsoever is presumably ironic in two senses. The jury would take him to be dissembling (the most common meaning of the Greek *eirōneia*), to be engaging in mock humility. But for Socrates the irony is probably more complex: he has no *divine wisdom* about anything, but does possess *human wisdom* in the sense he will outline shortly.

politicians that this happened to me. As I spoke with him it struck me that while this man *seemed* wise to many people, and especially to himself, he wasn't. And I then attempted to show him that although he believed that he was wise, he wasn't.

21d This, then, is why I came to be hated by this man and by many of those present.

But as I went off I thought to myself, 'I am wiser than this man, at any rate; probably neither of us knows anything admirable and good, but this man believes he knows something when he doesn't, while I – as I don't know it – don't believe that I do know. I probably am wiser than this man in this one, small respect: **I don't think I know what I don't know.**' Then I went off to another man, one of those who seemed even wiser than the first, and the same thing happened.

21e And thus I came to be hated by that man too, and by many others besides.

After this I moved on from one man to another, and had the painful and distressing realization that I was becoming hated. But it nevertheless seemed to me that it was necessary to consider the god's business of the highest importance. So I had to carry on going to everyone who seemed to know anything, as I examined what

22a the oracle meant. And, by **the dog**, gentlemen of Athens – for I must tell you the truth – this is what happened to me. It struck me, as I followed the god's lead and made my investigation, that those with the highest reputations were pretty much the worst off, while others who were considered less worthy were actually more knowledgeable men.

---

politicians the Greek word *politikos* refers to someone expert in matters having to do with the city (*polis*). 'Politician' can be misleading as a translation, though, since there were no professional politicians at Athens, as it was not possible to make a living by holding public office there (most offices were chosen by lot, and held only for one year). The term *politikos* applied to men who regularly took the lead in debates in the Athenian **Assembly**, whether they currently held office or not. Anytus, Socrates' most prominent prosecutor, was one such *politikos*.

I don't think I know what I don't know it thus emerges that Socrates' wisdom consists in his recognition of the limits of his knowledge. If you understand the limits of your knowledge, you must have some basic grasp of **epistemology**, the branch of philosophy devoted to understanding what counts as knowledge – and what doesn't. Socrates doesn't spell out any formal theory of epistemology here (or elsewhere), but we will see that to qualify as knowledge one must be able to explain what one is saying (something the poets cannot do), and that craftsmen provide us with at least one paradigm for what does count as knowledge. Socrates' ultimate goal is to know virtue as well as the craftsmen know their crafts; he never reaches this goal, which is why he can say, as he repeatedly does in the *Apology*, that he knows nothing important.

the dog is Anubis, a dog-headed god of Egypt. The oath 'by the dog', something of a favourite of Socrates, was old-fashioned and very mild. It here marks Socrates' pretended shock at discovering that politicians don't know anything.

22b My wanderings can only be described as **my labours** to show that I could not refute the oracle. After the politicians I went to **the poets – tragedians, dithyrambists, and the others –** as it was here that I would catch myself knowing less than they did. So whenever they recited the poems of theirs I thought were most carefully composed, I would ask them what they meant, **hoping to learn something from them along the way.** Well, I'm ashamed to tell you the truth, gentlemen, but it must be told. There was almost no one present who didn't have something better to say about the poems than the men who had composed them. I soon again recognized, then, that the poets did not do what they did through wisdom,

22c but **through some natural gift and out of inspiration**, like seers and those who produce oracles. For those people also say many admirable things, but don't understand anything they are saying. It became clear to me that this same sort of thing happens to poets as well. And at the same time I realized that they believed, because of their poetry, that they were the wisest of men about other things which they did not understand. So once again I came away believing that I was superior to them in the same way that I was superior to the others.

Finally, then, I went to the craftsmen. For I was aware that I knew almost nothing,

22d but I knew that I would discover that they, at least, knew many admirable things. In this I was not mistaken: they knew things which I did not and in this respect they were wiser than me. But, gentlemen of Athens, the good craftsmen seemed to me to make the same error the poets did. Because each of them had admirably

---

my labours   an allusion to Heracles, whose labours (and wanderings) Socrates compares to his own pursuit of the meaning of the oracle. Presumably Socrates wants to stress the Herculean efforts he made on behalf of the god; Heracles' labours were also undertaken under divine command. The comparison seems a bit of a stretch: Heracles defeated monsters all over the earth, while the mighty Socrates refuted various Athenians in Athens, only to show that he could not refute the oracle. A bit later on (**28c**, p. 55), Socrates will compare himself to Achilles. For more on Heracles, see pp. 117–23.

the poets – tragedians, dithyrambists, and the others   poets were regarded as educators, and their works were at the centre of Greek education; public speakers often quoted poetry, and many Presocratic philosophers wrote in verse. Dithyrambs were choral poems in honour of Dionysus, performed alongside tragedies at annual festivals of Dionysus.

hoping to learn something from them along the way   that is, Socrates hoped (he says) not only to discover men who knew more than he did, but to learn what they knew.

through some natural gift and out of inspiration   poets traditionally called upon the Muses for inspiration (as Homer does at the outset of his poems), but when Socrates says that someone works via poetic inspiration this sometimes appears to be a polite way of saying that he doesn't know what he is talking about. Philosophy aims to provide a surer foundation, though of course Socrates never fully succeeds in laying that foundation. For more on Socrates and poetic inspiration see Plato's *Ion*.

mastered his craft, he thought that he was also very wise about **other things, the most important ones**, and this mistake overshadowed the wisdom he did have.

22e So I asked myself, on behalf of the oracle, whether I would choose to stay as I am, neither wise where they are wise nor ignorant where they are ignorant, or to stay as I am in both respects. I answered myself, and the oracle, that I am better off as I am.

It's from these investigations, gentlemen of Athens, that a great deal of difficult
23a and deep-seated hatred has arisen against me, and this hatred has produced the slander against me and given me my reputation for wisdom. For when I refute someone about something, the people present believe that I am wise about the subject of the refutation. Actually, gentlemen, in reality it is probably the god who is wise, and with this oracle he is saying that human wisdom is worth little or
23b nothing. He appears to be talking about Socrates and using my name to make me an example, as if he were to say, 'The wisest of you human beings is the one who, like Socrates here, has recognized that he is in truth worthless when it comes to wisdom.'

---

other things, the most important ones Socrates does not clearly spell out here what these most important things are, but presumably they are the sorts of things politicians were thought to know, and the things that poets say admirable things about but can't explain. Later on (**29e**, p. 57), Socrates will say that the **soul** ought to be our most important concern, far more so than our bodies or our possessions. Caring for the soul means providing it with virtue; in the next chapter we will see how Socrates attempts to define the virtue of courage, a necessary step before we can be courageous, at least in Socrates' view. Unlike the politicians and poets, craftsmen have real knowledge; presumably they can not only produce fine products (as the poets can), but *explain* how to do so (as the poets cannot). While craftsmen are not wise in the most important sense, because their knowledge is limited to unimportant subject-matter, the crafts clearly provide an important model for how to characterize knowledge – they are a central part of Socratic epistemology. To be truly wise one would need to understand virtue as well as a good shoemaker understands shoes; this would require one not only to recognize virtue when one saw it (tough enough in the case of virtue), but to be able to produce it consistently, at least given the right materials (the mental equivalent of the shoemaker's leather), and to explain how to produce it. Socrates never reaches understanding of this level, and has never met anyone else with this knowledge; he concludes therefore that such knowledge is beyond mortals.

But Socrates does, as we will see, understand some things about virtue. He knows that a good man should not allow fear of death to prevent him from doing what is just (**28b**, p. 55) or lead him to disobey the commands of his betters (**29a–b**, p. 56). And he knows that a good man cannot be harmed (**30d**, p. 60). Such beliefs give Socrates the confidence to boldly reject the case against him. But Socrates' moral code does not amount to wisdom in the highest sense. One way Socrates' knowledge falls short is that he cannot give fully adequate explanations of what he does know about virtue, as he cannot produce fully satisfactory definitions of the virtues (as we'll see in chapter 3).

So even now, following the lead of the god, I continue to investigate these things and seek out anyone – whether he's from Athens or from out of town – who I think is wise. And if I decide he isn't wise, I come to the aid of the god and demonstrate that he is not. This keeps me so busy that I have no free time worth mentioning **to look after the affairs of the city** or my own affairs; instead, I am in 23c   **extreme poverty** through my service to the god.

What's more, the young who follow me about of their own accord, who have the most free time as they are sons of the very rich, delight in hearing other people being refuted, and themselves imitate me and so attempt to refute others. They then find, I believe, no shortage at all of people who believe that they know something, but actually know little or nothing. Now this leads those they refute 23d   to be angry with me instead of being angry at themselves, and to say that Socrates is a very nasty character who corrupts the young. Whenever someone asks them what I do or teach to corrupt the young, they don't know what to say, but to avoid appearing to be at a loss, they trot out the stock charges used against all

---

to look after the affairs of the city   at Athens, a prominent citizen could be criticized for not being active in public life. According to the historian Thucydides (*c.* 460–*c.* 400) the Athenian statesman **Pericles** said in his funeral oration of 431 BC that Athenians regard those who fail to take part in public affairs not as lacking in ambition but as useless (2.40.2). Socrates, as we have seen, served on the Athenian Council. Members of the Council were chosen by lot, but probably only from those who volunteered to serve (on the Council see **32b** on p. 62 and the text box on pp. 64–5). So Socrates did not shun all involvement in public life, just a leading role. At **36b** (p. 72) Socrates will explain his failure to take such a leading role.

extreme poverty   Socrates seems to have come from a reasonably well-off family but to have impoverished himself by neglecting his personal affairs and devoting himself to philosophy. Certainly Socrates looked poor: he went around barefoot and generally neglected his personal appearance (Plato, *Symposium* 174a). He spent most of his time in the company of the richest Athenians, however, and was able to benefit, at crucial moments, from the support of wealthy friends. Socrates will say later (**28e**, p. 56) that on three occasions from 432 to 422 he served as a **hoplite** (heavily armed infantryman; see also p. 86). Hoplites had to provide their own gear, which required a net worth of something around 20 minas; less than half of the citizens of Athens would have been that wealthy. At **38b** (p. 74), however, Socrates will say that he could manage to pay a fine of only one mina, and elsewhere Xenophon has him say that his property (including his house) was only worth five minas (*Oeconomicus* 2.3). His friends probably pitched in to enable him to serve as a hoplite, then, as they are willing to help him at his trial; at **38b** (p. 75) Socrates will note that they have volunteered to pay a fine of 30 minas on his behalf. So Socrates' poverty did not make him a man of the people, given his aristocratic connections; but it did clearly distinguish him from the sophists who grew rich by charging high fees for their services.

those who pursue philosophy: 'things up above and things beneath the earth', and 'not recognizing the gods', and 'making the weaker argument the stronger'. For they aren't willing, I think, to admit the truth: it's become obvious that they claim

23e to know, but actually know nothing. And because they are ambitious and energetic and numerous and have been speaking vigorously and persuasively about me, for a long time now your ears have been filled with their energetic slander.

It's on this basis that Meletus attacked me, as well as Anytus and Lycon; Meletus angry on behalf of the poets, **Anytus on behalf of the craftsmen and politicians,**

24a **and Lycon on behalf of the orators.** The result, as I said at the outset, is that I'd be amazed if I could counter this slander in such a short time, seeing that it has grown so great. This, gentlemen of Athens, is the truth, and I'm neither hiding nor glossing over anything great or small. I'm pretty sure that I've made myself more hated by what I've said just now – which is indeed evidence that what I've said is true. This slander against me has been caused by my saying this sort of

24b thing. Whether you look into this now or later, you'll find it's so.

---

those who pursue philosophy   the Greek term *philosophia* means 'love of wisdom'. Philosophy did not yet exist as a separate field, and the term referred to many sorts of intellectual activity. It was part of Plato's achievement, following in the footsteps of Socrates, to define philosophy both as a particular way of thinking and as a particular way of leading one's life. In the ancient view of things, a philosopher is not so much one who promotes a certain set of doctrines as one who devotes his life to investigation of the most fundamental questions. Socrates here appears to class not only himself but the sophists (who were attacked for 'making the weaker argument the stronger') and the Presocratics (who were attacked for atheism and investigating things above and below the earth) as philosophers, a rare admission that for all the differences between him and his controversial peers, they were all engaged in a similar quest for knowledge.

Anytus on behalf of the craftsmen and politicians   Anytus was a leading politician who inherited a successful tannery from his father; the tannery presumably explains why Socrates says he was upset on behalf of the craftsmen. For more on him, see the note at **18b**, p. 32.

Lycon on behalf of the orators   we know too little about Lycon to know why he acted on behalf of the orators (who may or may not be the same people as the politicians). Lycon's wife and his son were, like many other prominent Athenians, attacked in comedies for being promiscuous; the son, Autolycus, was beloved by the scandalous Callias (see the note at **20a**, p. 35). In Xenophon's *Symposium*, Socrates attempts to convince Callias not to have sex with Autolycus, but instead to devote himself to a nobler form of friendship. Lycon there praises Socrates (9.1), but may well do so hypocritically, as he himself was less severe with his son than Socrates was.

1 What might Socrates mean when he says (at **20e**, p. 38 above) that some sophists or Presocratics may have superhuman wisdom, while he himself has only human wisdom?

2 Does Socrates try to prove the oracle wrong, or to see how it can be right?

3 How does the oracle's response that no one was wiser than Socrates turn into a divine mission to question anyone in town who seems to know anything?

4 Do you think that poets and other creative artists work mainly by inspiration, rather than through some form of knowledge or skill?

5 Are you surprised when others can interpret creative work better than the creative artists themselves? What might explain this?

6 Socrates doesn't quite say that he knows nothing; he says that he knows nothing of the highest importance. As you read on, make note what Socrates appears to know. How does he know it? And is it really worth little or nothing?

7 Socrates prefers to know that he knows nothing important, rather than to be able to compose good poetry, or to master a craft, but lack this self-knowledge. Would you make the same choice? Why or why not?

8 Ancient rhetorical theory advised speakers to present themselves as credible and sympathetic individuals and their opponents as unreliable and unscrupulous villains. How does Socrates aim to show he is reliable, and his opponents unreliable? And how might his accusers have presented both sides differently?

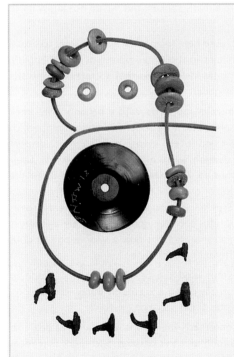

Simon the shoemaker

Archaeologists in Athens found these iron hobnails (used for giving tread to shoes) and bone eyelets in a building they identify as a shop, just off the edge of the Athenian agora (see map, p. 30). The circular black item, the base of a ceramic cup, was found nearby; it is labelled 'Simon's' (*Simonos* in Greek). Hence the identification of the shop as that of Simon the Shoemaker. **Diogenes Laertius** (2.122) tells us that Simon would take notes of conversations Socrates held in his shop, and was the first person to compose Socratic dialogues. Socrates often cites craftsmen like shoemakers as genuine experts, though not about the most important matters (as at *Apology* **22d**, p. 41). While Socrates sometimes speaks rather contemptuously of everyday Athenians, perhaps he frequented Simon's shop not only to meet other people but to chat with Simon himself.

Cup base, hobnails, and eyelets from the Athenian agora.

Corrupting the youth (24b–26a)

Let this be enough of a defence against the charges that the first accusers made against me. I'll next attempt to defend myself against Meletus, that good and patriotic man, as he says, and against **the later accusers**. Once again, as there is another set of accusers, let us take up their sworn statement. It goes something like

24c   this: *Socrates is guilty of **corrupting the youth** and of not recognizing the gods the city recognizes, but other **daimonic things** instead.*

That's how the charge goes; let us examine each part of it.

He says that I am guilty of corrupting the youth, but I, gentlemen of Athens, say that it is Meletus who is guilty, because he jokes around concerning a serious matter, and brings people to trial without a second thought, pretending to be serious and anxious about matters that have never been a **concern** to him. I will try to show you that this is the case.

---

the later accusers   are those behind the official charges against Socrates in 399: Meletus (who filed the official charges against Socrates), and Anytus and Lycon (who also spoke against him at the trial). These accusers have already spoken, but we do not know much about what they said.

corrupting the youth   while the Greek verb used here (*diaphtheirein*) can refer to sexual corruption, this connotation is not as prominent in the Greek phrase as it is in English. As we shall see, under questioning from Socrates Meletus says that Socrates corrupts the youth by teaching them false ideas about the gods.

daimonic things   (Greek *daimonia*) are things having to do with a **daimon**. The Greek noun *daimōn* can refer to a god, but can also refer to a lesser divinity or spirit which was not the object of religious worship like a god (Greek *theos*) was. Our word 'demon' is descended from the Greek daimon, but daimons were as often benign as evil. Later on (**27d**, p. 54), Socrates will say that daimons are considered either to be gods, or the offspring of gods and nymphs, or the offspring of gods and mortals. In Plato's *Symposium* (202d–203a), many of the speakers describe Eros (love) as a god, but Socrates treats Eros as a daimon, because Eros has an intermediate status between gods and mortals, and serves as a messenger between them. Greek religion included not only a wide range of gods (polytheism), but a considerable range of different types of divine being.

In his official charge against Socrates, Meletus used the term *daimonia* to allude to Socrates' divine sign, which in the Greek is usually called a 'daimonic thing' (*daimonion*). On Socrates' divine sign see pp. 19–20 in chapter 1 and **31c–e** on pp. 61–2.

concern   the Greek verb meaning 'to be concerned', *meletān*, sounds a great deal like Meletus' name, and Socrates puns on this throughout this passage. Such puns may seem flippant to us, but the study of word origins (etymology) was a rather serious business in Socrates' day: Plato has Socrates discuss etymology at length in the *Cratylus*.

24d 'Come here, Meletus, and tell me: don't you consider it of the utmost importance that the young become as good as they can be?'

'I do.'

'Come on, then, tell the men here: who makes the young better? Clearly you know, since this is a concern of yours. You've discovered who corrupts them – it's me, you say – and you're putting me on trial and accusing me. But come on, reveal who makes them better.

'Look, Meletus, you're silent and you have nothing to say! And doesn't this seem shameful to you, and an adequate proof of what I'm saying, that this has never been a concern of yours? Just tell us, my good man, how are the youth made better?'

'**The laws** do it.'

24e 'But I'm not asking what *thing* makes them better, Meletus, but rather what *person* – the person who will, in the first place, understand these very laws.'

'It's these people, Socrates – the jurors.'

'What do you mean, Meletus? Are these people able to educate the young and make them better?'

'Exactly.'

'Can all of them do so, or just some and not others?'

'All of them.'

'Well said, **by Hera**, that's certainly no shortage of benefactors! And what of this: 25a do **these people in the audience** make them better, or not?'

'These too.'

Come here, Meletus, and tell me   the two parties in an Athenian trial had the right to question one another.

The laws   are perhaps a bit less strange an answer in Greek than for us, as the Greek term (*nomoi*) can refer to customs and traditions as well as laws.

by Hera   Hera, the wife of Zeus, was most often invoked by women in oaths. 'By Hera' is nevertheless another favourite oath of Socrates (compare 'by the dog' at **22a**, p. 40). When used by a man, it can mark what he says as ironic, rather as a quaint exclamation like 'goodness gracious' does today. Socrates doesn't believe that all 500 of his jurors were capable of educating the young.

these people in the audience   Athenian trials were held in open-air courts, and many could gather around to listen to the proceedings; we will learn later (at **38b** on p. 75) that Plato and other friends of Socrates were among those observing the trial.

'And what about those serving on the **Council**?'

'The councillors, too.'

'Well then, Meletus, surely those in the **Assembly**, the Assemblymen, don't corrupt the youth, do they? Don't all of them also make them better?'

'These too.'

'So it seems that all Athenians make the young admirable and good, except for me, and that I alone corrupt them. Is this what you mean?'

'That's exactly what I mean.'

25b 'I'm very badly off indeed, according to you. Tell me this: does it work the same way with horses – it's everybody who makes them better, and just one person who corrupts them? Or is it completely the other way around – one man can make them better, or very few (the experts about horses), while most people, if they deal with horses, corrupt them? Isn't this the case, Meletus, not only for horses but for all animals? No doubt it's absolutely right, whether or not you and Anytus say it is. Our youth would be very well off indeed if only one person corrupted them,

25c while the rest benefited them. But actually, Meletus, you are demonstrating well enough that you've never given the youth any thought, and are clearly revealing your lack of concern: you've never concerned yourself with any of the things you are charging me with.

'By Zeus, Meletus, next tell us whether it is better to live among good fellow citizens or bad ones. Do answer, my good man – I'm not asking anything difficult. Don't bad men do some harm to those closest to them at any given time, while good men benefit them?'

'Of course.'

25d 'Now is there anyone who wants to be harmed by those around him rather than helped? Keep answering, my good man – for the law requires you to. Is there anyone who wants to be harmed?'

'Certainly not.'

Council   Every year, 500 Athenians were chosen by lot to serve on the Athenian Council (Greek *Boulē*), where they would prepare business for the Athenian Assembly (see the next note) and carry out a number of important supervisory and regulatory roles. For Socrates' service on the Council, see pp. 62–5.

Assembly   all adult male Athenian citizens could participate in the Assembly, the most important governmental body at Athens.

'Come, then, are you charging me today with intentionally corrupting the young and making them worse, or with doing it unintentionally?'

'I say it's intentionally.'

25e

26a

'How is this, Meletus? Are you so much wiser than I, despite being so much younger, that you have figured out that bad men always treat those nearest them badly, while good men treat them well, but I have grown so ignorant that I don't even know that whenever I put someone around me **in a bad way**, I run the risk of suffering some evil at his hands, with the result that, according to you, I intentionally do such great harm? I don't believe you about this, Meletus, and I think no one else does, either. No, either I do not corrupt, or, if I do corrupt, it's unintentional, so in either case you're wrong. If I corrupt them unwillingly, **this isn't the place the law assigns** for the prosecution of such mistakes; rather, you should take me aside in private and teach and reprimand me. For if I learn better, I will clearly stop doing this unintentionally. But you avoided meeting with me to teach me because you were unwilling to do so, and instead you prosecute me here, where the law orders one to prosecute those who need punishment, not those who need to be taught.'

---

in a bad way the Greek term here (*mochthēros*) originally referred to someone who was in a bad way because he was suffering hardship, but it came to be used of someone prone to treat others badly. Socrates uses this word to help him imply that if you treat someone badly, that person will become a bad person who will probably go on to treat others badly, including you. No one wants to be surrounded by harmful people, so no one can really want to treat others badly.

Now Socrates would presumably grant that some people (bad ones) *think* that they want to harm others, but this is only because they don't understand that what they're doing will ultimately hurt themselves. So their harmful actions aren't intentional in the most fundamental sense. In fact no one, Socrates would claim, wants to harm any other person; no one does wrong intentionally. This is one of the so-called **Socratic paradoxes**, moral claims that Socrates' contemporaries found difficult to believe, and that most of us find difficult to believe today. Another Socratic paradox is that virtue consists of knowledge: for anyone who knows the right thing to do unfailingly does it.

this isn't the place the law assigns Athenian law did draw a distinction between intentional and unintentional wrongdoing, but it certainly wasn't drawn on the philosophical grounds Socrates suggests here.

1 Missing from the list of those who improve the young at **24e–25a** (pp. 47–8) are parents and teachers. Why?

2 What does Socrates mean by 'harming the young'? Do most people really harm the young? Do most people harm animals – say, their pets, as Socrates implies?

3 Does harming people really make them harmful?

4 Socrates is terribly found of analogies, here the analogy between training animals and training people. Be on the look-out for them as you read on, and pause to consider how relevant the analogies are. How can you tell the difference between when an analogy helps to illustrate, or even prove, a given point, and when it misleadingly compares things that aren't really that comparable?

5 If Socrates is right, does anyone corrupt the youth intentionally? Does anyone harm anyone else intentionally? If not, what would we need law-courts for?

6 Is Socrates here trying to show that he is innocent? Or does he primarily want to show that Meletus has failed to give these matters any thought, and so has no business prosecuting him? Or could it be that his argument here is meant to show all of us that we – all too much like Meletus – don't know things we thought we knew about education and ethics?

Impiety as atheism (26b–28b)

26b 'Well, gentlemen of Athens, this much is already clear, as I was saying: these matters have never been of the slightest concern to Meletus. Nevertheless, Meletus, tell us, exactly how do you say that I corrupt the youth? Or isn't it clear that, **according to the indictment** you filed, I do so by teaching them not to recognize the gods the city recognizes, but other, new daimonic things? Aren't you saying that I corrupt them by teaching them this?'

'That's exactly what I'm saying.'

26c 'Then by these very gods that we're talking about, clarify this both for me and for these men here. For I don't understand whether you're saying that I teach the youth to recognize that some other gods exist, just not the ones the city recognizes, and it's this that you're accusing me of, of recognizing *other* gods – in which case

---

according to the indictment Socrates summarized the indictment at **24c** (p. 46). The indictment does not make clear how Socrates corrupted the youth, but as Socrates was charged under the law against impiety, the most relevant way of corrupting them would indeed be by spreading impious teachings, as Socrates and Meletus agree here.

I do recognize that gods exist and am not entirely godless and so am not guilty of that. Or do you say that I do not recognize any gods whatsoever and teach this to others?'

'That's what I say: **you don't recognize any gods whatsoever.**'

26d 'Meletus, you're amazing – why do you say this? Don't I recognize that **the sun and moon are gods**, as other people do?'

'No, by Zeus, he doesn't, gentlemen of the jury, since he says that the sun is a stone and the moon is made of earth.'

---

you don't recognize any gods whatsoever a crucial admission, since it allows Socrates to argue that he is innocent of the charge of impiety if he believes in any gods at all. Socrates in fact never says whether he believes in the gods of Athens. Moreover, Meletus' admission appears to contradict the precise wording of the charge, which both specifies that Socrates fails to recognize *the gods of the city* (not that he recognizes no gods at all) and says that he introduces some new sort of divinity.

Various theories have been put forth to explain Meletus' response here. Some think Meletus is a victim of tricky Socratic questioning, but Socrates' question here seems rather straightforward. Perhaps the law against impiety did define it as atheism, but we lack any evidence for this, and had the law defined it thus Socrates would hardly have needed to ask whether Meletus was charging him with atheism. Perhaps Meletus thought that no god not recognized in Athens was a real god. In logical terms, Meletus seems to have blown it, probably because, as Socrates repeatedly tells us, Meletus, unlike Socrates, hadn't really thought through what corrupting the youth meant. But of course Meletus won his case; so slandering Socrates with being an atheist may have done Socrates enough harm to mitigate any mistake Meletus made in allowing Socrates to change the terms of the debate to atheism.

What does it matter what Meletus thought? Some have argued that Meletus, as the official prosecutor, was the final authority on the meaning of the charges. But this is probably false: it was the jury that decided what the relevant law meant, and they were not bound by any interpretation Meletus gave. Remember that Athens had no separate judges or other legal professionals. Jurors were therefore free to convict Socrates even if he did prove that he wasn't an atheist, if they believed he was impious in other ways.

the sun and moon are gods both were indeed considered to be divinities. For example, people regularly swore oaths by the all-seeing Helios (sun), and the goddess Selene (the moon) was connected with Artemis, a goddess associated with women and childbirth. Scientific speculation about these celestial bodies could be dangerous. Socrates enters the *Clouds* looking down at the sun, and at the close of the play Strepsiades urges his slaves to beat Socrates and his followers because they had treated the gods with hubris (contempt; see the note at **27a**, p. 53) by investigating 'the seat of the moon' (1507).

'Do you think you're accusing **Anaxagoras**, my dear Meletus? And are you so contemptuous of the people here that you think they're illiterate and don't know that the books of Anaxagoras of Clazomenae are full of such talk? And no doubt it's from me that the young learn these things, although it's sometimes possible

26e
to **buy them in the showplace in the Agora for a drachma at most**, and they will laugh at Socrates, if he claims that they're his ideas – especially since they are so strange. Ah, by Zeus, is this what you think of me? That I don't recognize the existence of any god?'

'No, by Zeus, not a single one.'

'I don't think, Meletus, that you even believe this yourself. To me, gentlemen of Athens, he appears absolutely hubristic and out of control, and he has written up

---

Anaxagoras (*c.* 499–*c.* 428), from Clazomenae in Asia Minor (modern Turkey), was a Presocratic philosopher who did indeed attempt to explain celestial phenomena in terrestrial terms by saying the sun was a fiery stone and the moon was made of earth. Anaxagoras spent a good deal of his career at Athens, and may well have been put on trial for impiety, as Socrates would be later. But our sources for the trial are quite late and contradictory, which has led some to doubt that the trial ever took place. Anaxagoras was an associate of Pericles, a staunch proponent of democracy at Athens who was the most influential politician there for the thirty years before his death in 429. Anaxagoras may (if he was indeed put on trial) have been attacked by Pericles' political rivals. So too political motives may have contributed to the prosecution of Socrates, though in Socrates' case it was probably democrats who attacked him for his connections with enemies of democracy, while Pericles had been attacked by less democratic Athenian conservatives.

buy them in the showplace in the Agora for a drachma at most Socrates probably means that one could hear a talk on Anaxagoras' views for a drachma, rather than buy a copy of his book, which would probably have cost more than that, and would likely have been available more than occasionally if it was on sale. The 'showplace in the Agora' (the Greek term is *orchēstra*) was a place in the centre of the Agora where dramatic performances were held; it would also be a good place for an occasional lecture. Books were certainly more expensive in relative terms for Socrates' contemporaries than for us, and literacy rates were far lower, though literacy would have been the norm in the elite company Socrates kept. The 'illiteracy' Socrates has in mind here is that of someone who hadn't even heard of Anaxagoras' views; he implies that the average Athenian would have at least that much basic knowledge of Anaxagoras, just as the average person today knows something about Einstein.

27a this indictment simply out of his **hubris, shamelessness, and youth**. It's as if he's made a riddle to test us with: "Will Socrates the Wise figure out that I am joking around and contradicting myself, or will I fool him and the others who hear me?" To me it looks like he is contradicting his own indictment, just as if he were to say, "Socrates is guilty of not recognizing gods, but of recognizing gods." He's toying with us.

27b 'Consider, gentlemen, why he appears to me to be saying this. Meletus, you must answer us. And you, gentlemen, as I asked you at the beginning, remember not to interrupt if I conduct the conversation in my customary manner.

'Is there anyone, Meletus, who recognizes that there are human affairs, but doesn't recognize that humans exist? Let him answer now, gentlemen, and not just make a lot of confused objections. Is there anyone who does not believe that horses exist, but does believe in things having to do with horses, or who does not believe in flute-players, but does believe in things having to do with the flute? There's no one who does so, my fine fellow. If you don't want to answer, I'll say it for you and for the rest here. But at least answer this next question: is there anyone who **27c** believes in **daimonic things but doesn't believe in daimons**?'

'There isn't.'

'Oh, how helpful of you to answer, even if you do so reluctantly, and because the people here force you to do so. So you say that I both recognize and teach about daimonic things – no matter whether new or old, I do recognize some daimonic things, according to what you say, and you said as much under oath in the official indictment. But if I recognize daimonic things, surely I absolutely must also recognize daimons. Isn't that right? Yes, it is. I'll assume that you agree, since **27d** you won't answer. And don't we believe that daimons are gods or the offspring of gods? Yes or no?'

'Of course they are.'

---

hubris, shamelessness, and youth were closely associated terms at Athens. 'Hubris' in Greek referred not simply to overconfidence or arrogance but to behaviour intended to dishonour someone else, or to the state of mind that led to such behaviour. At Athens hubris could be a serious crime; prosecution was most common for assaults meant to humiliate and insult the victim and for cases of sexual assault, because they dishonoured not only the victims but the male guardians who were supposed to protect them. The young were thought to be prone to act this way – just as we see that crime rates today are highest among the young. Socrates is charging the young Meletus with courtroom hubris, with making a mockery of the legal process and the jury by presenting them with a riddle rather than a serious case.

daimonic things but doesn't believe in daimons for the meaning of these terms, see the note at **24c** on p. 46.

'So if I believe in daimons, as you say, and daimons are a sort of god, this is where I say you are riddling and joking around: you say that I don't believe in gods and then turn around and say I do believe in them, inasmuch as I believe in daimons. And if daimons are the children of gods, illegitimate children by **nymphs** or someone else, who in the world would believe that children of gods exist, but gods don't? That's just as absurd as believing in mules, the offspring of horses and donkeys, but not believing in horses and donkeys. No, Meletus, you must be testing us by filing this indictment, because you weren't able to charge me with any real injustice. There's absolutely no way you could persuade anyone who has any sense at all that one and the same person believes in daimonic and divine things, but doesn't believe in daimons, gods, or **heroes**.

27e

28a

'Well then, gentlemen of Athens, I don't think a long speech is required to show that I'm innocent of what Meletus' indictment charges me with; this much should do. But you can be sure of the truth of what I was saying earlier: many men have come to hate me, and to hate me a great deal. And it is this that will convict me, if I am convicted, not Meletus or Anytus but the slander and envy of the majority. This has convicted **many other good men too**, and I believe it will convict others to come. There's no reason to fear that it will stop with me.'

28b

---

1 Meletus' decision to claim that Socrates was an utter atheist has puzzled many, as it seems to contradict the wording of his own indictment of Socrates (see the note at **26c** on p. 51). But he won his case. So was it a wise move to claim that Socrates was a complete atheist, even if doing so was logically inconsistent?

2 Socrates proves that anyone who believes in the daimons recognized by most Greeks must also believe in gods. But does Socrates' argument tell us anything at all about what he himself believes?

3 Socrates never explicitly says that he believes in the gods of Athens. Why not?

4 Would you, as a juror, believe a defendant who uses a logical argument to prove that he is innocent, but is unwilling to come out and say that he is innocent himself?

---

nymphs   are female divinities associated with various elements in the natural world – trees, rivers, mountains, etc. They are sometimes said to be immortal, sometimes merely extremely long lived, and often appear as mothers of gods or heroes.

heroes   were dead men who retained powers after death, and were sometimes worshipped. In myth they were often said to be sons of a god and a mortal.

many other good men too   Socrates may be thinking of mythological examples (see **41b** on p. 79), of recent cases of prosecution of intellectuals like Anaxagoras (see the note at **26d**, p. 52), or of cases in which prominent politicians (among them his own associate **Alcibiades**) were punished by Athenian courts.

Socrates, the new Achilles (28b–30c)

Well, perhaps someone will say, 'So aren't you ashamed, Socrates, to have devoted yourself to something that could now get you killed?' Here's the right reply for me to make to him: 'That's no noble thing to say, sir, to believe that a man of any use whatsoever should, in whatever he is doing, factor in whether he will live or die, and not instead focus on this one thing: whether what he's doing is just or unjust,

28c   the deed of a good man or of a bad one. To your way of thinking the heroes who met their ends at Troy would be worthless, especially the **son of Thetis**. He scorned danger rather than submitting to anything disgraceful. As he was intent on killing Hector, his mother, a goddess, told him **something like this, as I recall**: *My child, if you do avenge the death of Patroclus and kill Hector, you yourself will die, for after Hector your fate awaits you at once.* When he heard this, he thought little of death and danger, but was far more afraid of living a coward's life by

28d   not avenging his friends. *At once may I die*, he says, *after inflicting justice on that wrongdoer, so that I do not remain here as a laughing-stock among the beaked ships, a burden to the land.* You don't believe that he thought much of death and danger, do you?'

For this is how it is, gentlemen of Athens, in truth. Whenever someone takes a stand, in the belief that it is the best position for him to hold, or whenever a commander assigns someone a position to maintain, there he must, it seems to me, hold his ground and face the danger, accounting neither death nor anything else more important than disgrace. I, then, would have done something terrible,

28e   gentlemen of Athens, if I stood my ground like the rest and faced the risk of

---

son of Thetis   Achilles, the son of Thetis, a sea goddess, and the mortal Peleus, was the greatest of the Greek warriors in the Trojan war. Homer's *Iliad* tells the tale of his withdrawal from the fight at Troy, due to his anger at being dishonoured by the leader of the Greeks, Agamemnon, and of his return to battle to avenge the death of his friend, Patroclus. Though Homer does not depict the death of Achilles, he does make it clear, as we'll see, that Achilles' decision to kill Hector meant that he was destined to die at Troy.

something like this, as I recall   Plato has Socrates loosely quote and paraphrase from Homer, *Iliad* 18.95–8. Homer's *Iliad* and *Odyssey* (dating to roughly 750 and 725 BC respectively) were central to Greek education, and well-educated Athenians would know much of Homer by heart. Homer's poems were admired not only for their poetry but for the values they taught. Loose quotations would be normal enough in a primarily oral culture, but Plato here has Socrates intentionally alter Homer's text to make his point clearer. Among other differences, Homer's Achilles says nothing of justice or wrongdoing. There was nothing immoral about Hector's killing Patroclus on the field of battle. But Achilles does choose to avenge his friend's death knowing full well that it will lead to his own, and the willingness to risk or even choose death was as heroic then as now.

---

death when I was positioned at **Potidaea and Amphipolis and Delion** by the commanders **whom you appointed** to give me commands, but then when the god gave me the command, as I believe and understand that he has done – that I had to live a life in the pursuit of wisdom by examining both myself and others – I then feared death or any other thing and deserted my post. Yes, that would be terrible, and then one could justly bring me to court because I did not recognize the existence of the gods, disobeyed the oracle, feared death, and believed that I was wise when I was not.

For to fear death, gentlemen, is nothing other than to seem wise when one is not, for it is to think one knows what one does not. For all we know, death may really be the greatest of all goods for mankind; but people fear it as if they knew that it was the greatest of evils. And how is this not the most reprehensible sort of ignorance, to believe one knows what one does not? Here too, gentlemen, I perhaps differ from most people, and if I were to claim some wisdom beyond that of most men, this is what it would be: as I do not know enough about **the things in Hades**, so also I do not believe that I do know. But to do injustice and disobey my better, god or man, this I know to be bad and disgraceful. And never will I fear or flee from things which may, for all I know, be good, rather than from the things I know to be evil.

29a

29b

Potidaea and Amphipolis and Delion battles fought by Athens in 432–430, 422, and 424 as part of the **Peloponnesian War** (431–404) she and her subjects waged against Sparta and her allies. At Potidaea Socrates distinguished himself by saving the life of Alcibiades, as Plato has Alcibiades himself tell us (Plato, *Symposium* 219e–220e; for more on Alcibiades, see chapter 1, p. 14); at Delion Socrates' bravery during the Athenian retreat led the general Laches to say that the Athenians would have won the battle had the rest of the Athenians been as brave as Socrates (Plato, *Laches* 181b; see also Plato, *Symposium* 221a–c).

whom you appointed Athenian generals were elected by the citizens of Athens (unlike most Athenian public officials, who were selected by a lottery: see pp. 13–14), and Socrates, like other speakers before Athenian popular juries, routinely identifies his jurors with the citizenry as a whole.

the things in Hades in popular belief, formed to a large extent by Homer's poetry (especially *Odyssey* book 11), the dead were thought to live on in an attenuated form, without much sensation or knowledge of what was going on around them. Some mystery rites offered initiates a better afterlife, but there was nothing as clear-cut as heaven and hell are in conventional Christian theology. Here as elsewhere – though Socrates' own case is an important exception – Greek religion did not impose a set of dogmas all pious people were supposed to share. So Socrates' ignorance of the afterlife would not have seemed strange to his contemporaries.

29c Perhaps you would be prepared to acquit me now, disregarding **Anytus, who said** that either I should never have been brought to court in the first place, or, given that I had been, that there was no alternative other than to kill me, for if I escaped, your sons would practise what Socrates teaches and all be completely corrupted. So suppose you said to me, 'Socrates, we will not listen to Anytus, but instead will let you go for now, upon the following condition: that you no longer continue in this search or pursue wisdom, and if you are caught doing this, you shall die.'

29d If you were to let me go on these terms, this is what I would say to you.

'Gentlemen of Athens, I'm very fond of you indeed, but I will listen to the god rather than to you, and as long as I draw breath and I am able to do so, I will not stop pursuing wisdom and exhorting you and showing the way to any of you I meet, speaking in my usual words:

"Best of men, you are an Athenian, and **your city is the greatest and most glorious in wisdom and in power**; are you not ashamed that while you concern yourself

29e with having as much money as possible, and as much glory and honour, you are so unconcerned about knowledge and truth and making your **soul** the best that it can be that you do not give these things a second thought?"'

Anytus, who said   presumably Anytus said this at the trial. Both the official prosecutor (here Meletus) and the defendant (Socrates) could have others address the jury on their behalf, in addition to speaking themselves. Presumably Lycon (see **24a**, p. 44) also spoke against Socrates; we do not know if others spoke on Socrates' behalf. Anytus' remark seems to show a wise recognition that putting Socrates on trial gave Socrates a public platform from which he could teach – and hence corrupt – many more of the youth than he would have reached otherwise. Better then either to ignore him, limiting his impact, or silence him forever: a lesser verdict would only gain Socrates publicity. Socrates made such good use of his opportunity that he is even today still teaching (corrupting?) us through his speech.

your city is the greatest and most glorious in wisdom and in power   this had indeed been true for most of Socrates' life. But in 399, as Socrates spoke at his trial, Athens' power had been broken. And the golden age of Athenian culture had ended; there would be no more great tragedy or comedy in Athens, nor was there any longer much patronage for ambitious architecture. But philosophy, inspired in large part by Socrates himself (via his student Plato and Plato's student **Aristotle**), would be Athens' living claim to fame.

soul   in classical Greek the soul (Greek *psychē*) is that which gives life, and is the seat of emotions, of thought and of the virtues; it thus also includes what we would call the mind. The soul is often contrasted with the body, or with external possessions like wealth or glory, the contrasts at issue here. It is not primarily a religious conception, as the term 'soul' so often is in English. In contemporary language, one might translate Socrates' point as follows: 'care not about wealth or fame, but about being the best person you can be'.

'And whenever one of you disputes this and says that he does concern himself with these things, I will not let him off easily, but I will question him and examine him and I will refute him, and if it appears to me that he does not possess virtue, but says that he does, I will reproach him because he treats what is most worthy as least important, and treats what is of less worth as if it mattered more.

30a

'This I will do for young and old, anyone I meet, foreigner and citizen – though more so for the citizens, as you are closer to me by birth. The god gives me this command, you can be sure, and I believe that there has never yet been any greater good for you in this city than my service to the god. I go around doing nothing else than persuading you, both young and old, not to put care for your bodies or your money before the utmost care that your soul be as good as it can be, and I say, "It is not from money that virtue comes, but from virtue that money and all other good things come both to individuals and to the people as a whole."

30b

'If by saying this I corrupt the youth, it's this that would be harmful. And if anyone claims I say something other than this, he's speaking nonsense. As far as this goes,' I would say, 'either listen to Anytus or not, gentlemen of Athens, either release me or not, knowing that I will not do otherwise, no, not even if I am to die many times over.'

30c

---

1 How can Socrates, who has just stressed that he knows nothing important, so emphatically say that he knows that it is wrong to disobey one's superior or act unjustly?

2 Socrates says that he does not know what awaits him after death, and that it is foolish to fear the unknown. Why does he think it is foolish to fear the unknown? Do you fear what comes after death?

3 Are Socrates' 'usual words' to the average Athenian (**29d–30a**, pp. 57–8) the sorts of things that you thought he would say as he examined people? If not, how does he come to consider them part of his divine mission?

4 Do you think that Socrates' imagined speech to the Athenians (starting at **29d**, p. 57) would have won a positive response? Would the praise of Athens have put them on his good side, or would he irritate them by claiming that they fail to pay attention to what really matters?

5 Socrates appears to allow for something like civil disobedience when he says that he would obey the god rather than the jury were the jury to order him to stop philosophizing. Does he give us any guidance on when civil disobedience is justified?

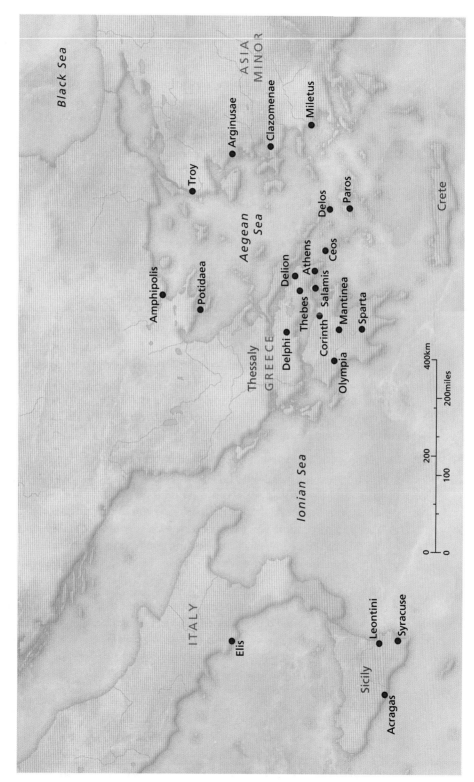

The Greek world in Socrates' day.

Socrates the gadfly (30c–31c)

Don't interrupt, gentlemen of Athens, but respect my request that you keep quiet and listen to what I am saying. For you will, I believe, profit from what you hear. Now I am indeed about to say some other things that may make you want to shout out. Yet by no means do so, for you can be sure that if you kill such a man as I say I am, you will not harm me more than you harm yourselves. Meletus (not to mention Anytus) won't do me any harm; he's not able to do so. For I believe that **it is ordained** that a better man cannot be harmed by a worse one. Yes, he may perhaps kill me or exile me or strip me of my citizenship. He may believe that these are great evils, as many others do, but I do not believe that this is so; no, it's far worse to do what he's doing, to attempt to kill a man unjustly.

30d

So, gentlemen of Athens, I'm far from speaking in my own defence, as one would expect me to; rather I'm defending you, so that you will not make a mistake about the gift of the god by condemning me. For if you kill me, you will not easily find another such as me, one whom the god has attached to the city, which is like a large thoroughbred horse that is rather sluggish owing to its size and needs to be woken up by a **gadfly** (the comparison is just right, even if somewhat droll). The god has placed me in the city like this, to wake you up and persuade and rebuke each one of you, continually landing all over you all the day long. Another such man you won't easily find, gentlemen, so if you listen to me, you'll spare me. But perhaps you will be irritated, and, like those who are woken up when they are nodding off, you may swat me, listening to Anytus, and kill me without a thought, to spend the rest of your lives slumbering away – unless the god, in his concern for you, sends you someone else.

30e

31a

Here's how you can tell that I really am the sort of man who has been sent by the god. It is hardly human nature for me to fail to be concerned with any of my own business and to ignore my personal affairs for so many years, but always to be minding your business, coming up to each of you in private like a father or older brother and persuading you to concern yourselves with virtue. If I got something out of this, or took some pay for exhorting you in this way, then it would make a certain sense. But as it is, you yourselves can see that even my accusers, for all the

31b

---

it is ordained   a Socratic paradox. Socrates thus claims that it is somehow part of the order of things, an order presumably established by the gods, that a better man cannot be harmed by a worse one. But this is no ordinary claim that most would agree with, as Socrates indicates by saying that the jury may object to what he says. Socrates must radically redefine the meaning of better and worse to give them his particular ethical sense: to be better is to be more just, and ordinary punishments (death, exile, etc.) do not make one less just and thus do no real harm, in Socrates' sense. Compare **41d** (p. 80), where Socrates says that a good man cannot be harmed at all.

gadfly   a type of fly that preys on large mammals, including humans; they are also known as horse flies or deer flies. This passage is the origin of the metaphor of the 'social gadfly' who irritates people into rethinking their beliefs.

other shameless accusations they have made, weren't shameless enough to find a witness to say that I ever took any pay or even asked for it. For I provide an adequate witness to the truth of what I'm saying, I believe: **my poverty**.

> 1 Socrates claims that it is ordained, it is somehow part of the order of things, that a bad man cannot harm a good one. What kind of divine order would justify this claim? And what evidence might Socrates have for this sort of divine order? Do you think good people can be harmed by bad ones?
>
> 2 Why does Socrates choose to compare himself to such a nasty insect?
>
> 3 If the gods sent us a gadfly today, what would that gadfly tell us?

Why Socrates stays out of politics (31c–33b)

Now it may perhaps seem strange that I go about giving this advice and making a nuisance of myself in private, but do not dare **to come forward and address the majority of you** to give advice to the city. The cause of this is something you have often heard me talking about, and in many places: something **divine and daimonic** comes to me, the very thing that Meletus, as if he were a comic poet, mocks in his indictment. This has happened to me since I was a boy – **a certain voice** comes to me, and whenever it comes, it always turns me away from what I am about to do, and never turns me towards anything. It is this which has opposed

---

my poverty   see the note on **23c** (p. 43).

to come forward and address the majority of you   one would do so at a meeting of the Athenian Assembly, the most important body in the Athenian government, which met in an open-air meeting place on the hill known as the Pnyx, south-west of the Acropolis. 'The majority of you' here refers to the Athenian people gathered in the Assembly. See the note at **23b** (p. 43) for the expectation that someone as prominent as Socrates would take an active part in public life. Socrates' poverty would not have prevented him from doing so. Any male citizen, no matter how poor, could participate in the Assembly, and while the Athenians did not start to pay citizens to attend the Assembly until after Socrates' death, Socrates was hardly too busy making a living to talk about the prominent issues of the day.

divine and daimonic   that is, something connected with god and with a daimon, a lesser divinity; Socrates here uses 'divine and daimonic' together to indicate that he is unaware of the precise origin of his experience, but knows that it is superhuman in some sense. For the meaning of 'daimonic' and its use in the charge against Socrates, see the note at **24c** on p. 46.

a certain voice   Socrates' divine sign is one of the most mysterious things about him. At least in Plato, the voice always says no and never says yes; but it comes often enough that its failure to appear allows Socrates to draw the conclusion that he is on the right track (see **40a–c**, p. 78). The sign itself is not a divinity, but it presumably comes from some daimon, some god, or the gods in general – Socrates isn't sure. Both Plato and Xenophon indicate that the sign played a large role in Socrates' being suspected of impiety; see chapter 1, pp. 19–20.

31e my getting involved in politics – and it's a very good thing that it has opposed me, it seems to me. For you can be sure, gentlemen of Athens, that if I had tried to get involved in politics long ago, I would long ago have perished without doing you or myself any good. Don't be upset with me for speaking the truth. For no one will survive if he **nobly opposes you or any other multitude**, and tries to prevent many injustices and illegalities from happening in the city; one who is to really

32a fight on behalf of justice, if he is to survive for even a short time, must do so as a private citizen rather than in public life.

I will provide you with substantial evidence of this – not mere words, but the thing you honour, deeds. Hear, then, what has happened to me, and learn that I will never, through fear of death, give in to anyone when it is unjust to do so, never giving in even if I would perish at once. What I will tell you are **things all too commonly boasted of in court**, but this is the truth. I, gentlemen of Athens,

32b never held any public office, but **did serve on the Council**. It so happened that

---

nobly opposes you or any other multitude   Plato's Socrates is highly critical of Athenian democracy. Many Athenian aristocrats, members of the sort of old, rich families that once dominated political life in Athens and still dominated the political life in most cities in Greece, were rather contemptuous of the multitude, the common people who had such a large say at Athens. Aristocrats believed that the common people were not educated enough to make sound political choices (there was, essentially, no public education in Athens or any other Greek city); the majority of people, aristocrats believed, were so poor that they were enslaved to their own pressing needs, and were therefore incapable of looking to the long-term interests of the city. Many Athenian aristocrats nevertheless continued to play an active role in public life. But others resentfully abandoned the leading public role their ancestors had played to pursue their own interests, and what they thought was best for the city, through private and non-democratic means. Some ended up plotting against the Athenian democracy, which was briefly overthrown, twice, during Socrates' lifetime (in 411 and 404). Socrates' associate Alcibiades was implicated in the first of these plots and his associate **Critias** was a leader of the second. So Socrates' abstention from political life was doubly suspicious. He was obviously interested in political issues, but refused to take a leading part in public, democratic debate; and some of his followers were clearly anti-democratic.

things all too commonly boasted of in court   speakers in Athenian trials often spoke of their past public service to the city, or their unwillingness to meddle in private affairs that did not concern them. Socrates can boast instead of his unwillingness to go along with public misconduct. Athenian trials were as much judgements on the whole life and character of the man on trial (and only men could appear in court) as on the merits of the particular case at hand.

did serve on the Council   for Socrates' service on the Council, and how Council service worked, see the text box on pp. 64–5.

32c our tribe, Antiochis, provided the presiding committee when you wanted to judge the ten generals who had not recovered the men **from the naval battle**, and to do so all together at once – illegally, as all of you came to see later on. At that time I alone of those on the presiding committee opposed your doing anything contrary to the laws, and I voted against you. Though the popular speakers were ready to charge and arrest me at once, and you were shouting for me to do it, I believed that I had to face the danger to the end, taking the side of law and justice, rather than, out of fear of imprisonment or death, taking your side when you wanted to do injustice.

32d And that was when the city was still democratic. But when **the oligarchy** took over, the Thirty had me brought to the **Tholos**, with four others, and ordered us to bring **Leon of Salamis** from Salamis so that he could be killed. This is the sort of thing they ordered many others to do on many occasions, as they wanted to make as many as possible complicit in their crimes. Note that then again I showed not in word but in deed that death, to put it a bit bluntly, is no concern at all to me: my only concern is avoiding anything unjust or unholy. That regime did not compel me, strong though it was, to do anything unjust, but when we left the Tholos, the other four went off to Salamis and brought back Leon, but I went off home. I might well have been killed for doing this, had the regime not fallen

32e quickly. Many can provide you with evidence of these things.

33a So do you think that I could have survived for so many years had I practised politics and done so in a way worthy of a good man, had I come to the defence of justice and regarded this the most important thing to do, as one should? Far from it, gentlemen of Athens. Nor could any other man whatsoever. No, through the whole of my life, in public affairs (whenever I engaged in them) and private ones, it will be clear that I was always the same man, one who never gave in to anyone

---

from the naval battle   Arginusae, fought in 406; see the text box on pp. 64–5.

the oligarchy   the Thirty Tyrants, the pro-Sparta junta that ruled Athens briefly from the autumn of 404 until the spring of 403.

Tholos   a circular building in the Athenian Agora that, under the democracy, housed the presiding committee of the Athenian Council. The Thirty made it their headquarters during their rule. See the map on p. 30.

Leon of Salamis   was a highly regarded Athenian general who was closely aligned with the democratic faction at Athens, and was hence a natural target for the oligarchic Thirty Tyrants. Salamis is an island just off the coast of Athens; the narrow strait between Athens and Salamis was the site of the great Greek naval victory over the Persians in 480 BC. See the map on p. 59.

when this was unjust, including any of **those who my slanderers claim were my students**. And I was never anyone's teacher. Whenever anyone desires to hear me speaking and doing what I do, I never begrudge this to anyone, young or old, nor do I speak with someone if he gives me money, but not speak with him if I don't get any. Rather, I make myself available to anyone, rich or poor, to question me, and, if he wants, to hear what I have to say in reply. It's not right to hold me responsible if any of these people turns out well or not, for I neither promised to teach anyone anything, nor did I in fact teach anything. If someone says that he ever learned anything from me or heard from me in private something that everyone else hasn't heard, you can be sure that he's not telling the truth.

The Arginusae scandal

In 406 an Athenian fleet defeated a Spartan fleet near the Arginusae islands off the coast of what is now Turkey. But when a storm blew up after the battle, the commanders of the fleet failed to recover Athenian sailors left floating among the wreckage; it is not clear whether this was largely a matter of rescuing the living or of recovering the bodies of the dead, but even the latter was an important failure. This failure was held against the generals in command, rightly or wrongly, but our sources are clear that the procedure used against them was contrary to Athenian law, which mandated that those charged on capital crimes be given separate trials. Instead all of the generals were condemned at once by a single vote of the Assembly, with no formal trial at all.

Meetings of the Assembly were run by a presiding committee (the *prytaneis*) drawn from the Athenian Council. Council members were selected by lot, apparently from all those citizens willing to serve. Fifty men were chosen from each of the ten groups into which all Athenian citizens were divided, the 'tribes' of Athens. One could serve as a Councillor twice, but even so the need to have 500 citizens serve each year, out of a citizen population of no more than 30,000, made this service something that may well have been considered part of the normal course of citizenship: hence Socrates can say he did not 'do politics' despite serving as a Councillor.

---

those who my slanderers claim were my students   an apparent reference to Critias, a leader of the Thirty; the renegade democrat Alcibiades may also be meant. These are the two associates of Socrates who would have been powerful enough to ask him to yield to them unjustly. Plato's Socrates consistently claims not to have taught anyone anything. This is one of his paradoxical ironies: it is true that Socrates did not take pay for teaching, and did not give lectures meant to pass on information in a straightforward way. But of course by asking probing questions he helped many, including Plato – who of course wrote this very passage – to learn a great deal indeed.

Each tribe's contingent served as the presiding committee for one-tenth of the year. Socrates was on the Council this year, and it was Socrates' tribe, Antiochis, that happened to be serving as the presiding committee when the Arginusae affair was debated. It appears that Socrates was the very man chosen by lot to be the chairman running the meeting (*epistatēs*). We are told that Callixenus, who here leads the attack on the generals, was subsequently prosecuted for his role in this affair. Here's an account of the key moment from Xenophon, the historian and follower of Socrates.

> Euryptolemus and some others made a motion against Callixenus, saying that he had proposed an illegal indictment [to condemn the generals without proper trials]. Some of the people praised this, but the majority shouted out that it would be a terrible thing if someone did not allow the people to do whatever they wanted. When Lysiscus added that these men should be judged by the same vote as the generals if they did not withdraw their motion, the mob shouted out again, and forced them to withdraw it. When some of those on the presiding committee said they would not agree to put the matter to a vote contrary to the law, Callixenus rose again and made the same charges against them. The people shouted that those who refused would be prosecuted. Those on the presiding committee took fright and agreed to have a vote – all save for Socrates son of Sophroniscus. He said that he would not do so, but would do everything according to the law. Then Euryptolemus took the platform and spoke in defence of the generals.
>
> (Xenophon, *History of Greece*, 1.7.12–16)

- It seems amazing to us that Socrates happened to be the chairman of the Athenian Assembly on the day of such an important crisis. But given that Athens had a different chairman every day, and that the office could be held only once, as many as one in four (male) Athenian citizens may have held that office at some point in their lives. The Assembly that condemned the Arginusae generals would itself have been made up of 6,000 citizens, at least one in five of the citizens of Athens. Would this high level of citizen involvement make politics more dangerous and unjust – or less so?

- During the Arginusae affair, Socrates refused to act illegally, but he did not speak out himself against those acting illegally, leaving this to Euryptolemus. Similarly, Socrates refused to participate in the murder of Leon of Salamis, but did nothing to stop it from taking place. He didn't try to warn Leon, or to convince the Thirty, or the other men sent to kill Leon, not to kill him. Does this lessen his heroism? Or is it justifiable in some way?

- Do you think you can be successful in politics today without sacrificing your principles?

- Some today have argued that our democracies should be more direct, perhaps by using new technology to allow all citizens a greater participatory role. What lessons might the trial and life of Socrates teach us about such efforts?

Socrates' true associates (33b–34b)

33c   Why then is it that some enjoy spending a great deal of time with me? You've heard why, gentlemen of Athens; I've told you the whole truth. They enjoy listening when people who believe they are wise, but aren't, are refuted: it isn't unpleasant. I myself have been commanded to do this, I maintain, **by the god both in oracles and in dreams** and in every other way in which the divine has ever transmitted its dispensation to anyone.

33d   These things, gentlemen of Athens, are both true and easy to verify. For if I am corrupting some of the youth and have already corrupted others, surely some of them, now that they are older, ought to come forward now themselves, accuse me, and take their revenge, if they have come to see that when they were young I gave them some bad advice. And if they themselves are unwilling to do so, then members of their families – fathers or brothers or other relatives – if indeed members of their families were harmed by me, ought to bring this to our attention and take their revenge.

33e   At any rate I see many of them present here: first **Crito here, my old friend and neighbour**, father of Critobulus over there; next Lusanias from Sphettus, father

---

by the god both in oracles and in dreams   'oracles' presumably refers to the Delphic oracle (**20c–23c** on pp. 38–43). For the dreams (a standard way for the gods to communicate to men in Greek thought) see Plato, *Phaedo* 60e–61a, where Plato has Socrates report that he often dreamt that a figure came to him and told him to make music. In the past, Socrates took this to mean that he ought to continue doing what he was already doing, philosophy; 'music' in Greek refers to anything inspired by the Muses, so could include philosophy. But in prison he began to take the dream more literally, and wrote a hymn to Apollo and then set some of Aesop's fables to verse. These are, as far as we know, the only things that Socrates wrote himself.

Crito here, my old friend and neighbour   Socrates literally calls Crito 'a man of my own age and a fellow demesman'. Crito and Socrates were assigned to the same neighbourhood (**deme**) in Athens, Alopeke; all Athenian citizens were registered into the home deme of their ancestors, and the deme structure formed the basis of Athenian political units. It is Crito who tries to convince Socrates to escape from prison in Plato's *Crito*; he is also the man Socrates calls upon to take care of his corpse at the end of Plato's *Phaedo*. Crito himself appears to have been a steady conventional Athenian who prospered as a farmer; his son, Critobulus, was somewhat wild, at least as a youth, and his father evidently hoped that Socrates could improve him. Critobulus often speaks with Socrates in Xenophon, but it is not clear that Socrates had any success in changing his ways.

---

of **Aeschines**; and Antiphon from Cephisia, father of **Epigenes**. Then there are those whose brothers were associates of mine: Nicostratus, son of **Theozotides** and brother of Theodotus (Theodotus is dead, so he, at any rate, cannot ask his brother to lie on his behalf); and Paralius here, son of Demodocus, whose brother

34a was **Theages**. And there is Adeimantus, son of Ariston, whose brother **Plato** is here, and Aeantodorus, brother of **Apollodorus** over there. And I could name many others, all of whom Meletus ought to have called as witnesses during his speech. If he forgot to do so, let him do it now – I yield the floor to him; let him speak up if he has any evidence of this sort. But you'll discover that quite the opposite is true, gentlemen, that all of these men are ready to come to the aid of the one who did the corrupting, the one who – according to Meletus and Anytus – did wrong to

34b their relatives. It's true that those who were themselves corrupted **may have some reason to come to my aid**. But as for their relatives, who were not corrupted since they were already mature men, what reason would they have to aid me, other than an upright and just one – they know that Meletus is lying, and that I am telling the truth?

Aeschines wrote Socratic dialogues which were highly regarded in antiquity, but only fragments of his writings survive. Sphettus was his home deme in Attica. This Aeschines is often called Aeschines Socraticus or Aeschines of Sphettus to distinguish him from the orator named Aeschines who was active some 50 years later.

Epigenes was also present at Socrates' death; otherwise we meet him only as the recipient of some advice on physical fitness from Socrates in Xenophon (*Memorabilia* 3.12). Cephisia is his deme.

Theozotides was a prominent democratic leader; Socrates' connection with his son, Theodotus, could thus have won him some sympathy among the jurors.

Theages is said to have had the potential for a political career, had his poor health not turned him towards philosophy instead, much as Socrates' divine sign turned him away from politics (Plato, *Republic* 6.496b). His father Demodocus was a prominent general.

Plato refers to himself only three times in his dialogues. The other two occasions come at **38b** on p. 75, where he volunteers to pitch in to help pay a fine for Socrates, and at *Phaedo* 59b, where we are told that Plato was sick and so was not present for Socrates' death. Socrates here suggests that Adeimantus, as Plato's eldest brother, would have complained had Socrates corrupted Plato; but Adeimantus was himself a companion of Socrates, and is, together with Plato's other brother, Glaucon, one of Socrates' main speaking partners in Plato's *Republic*.

Apollodorus was perhaps the closest thing Socrates had to a groupie; he was terribly enthusiastic but perhaps not terribly intelligent (see Plato, *Symposium* 172c–173a; Xenophon, *Apology* 28). Plato depicts Apollodorus as the most emotional of Socrates' followers at the scene of Socrates' death (Plato, *Phaedo* 117d).

may have some reason to come to my aid anyone corrupted by Socrates presumably wouldn't want to admit that he had been corrupted, and so would instead defend Socrates – and ask his relatives to do likewise. Socrates noted as much when remarking just above that one of his associates, Theodotus, is dead and therefore cannot ask his relatives to lie on his behalf.

Closing of the main speech (34b–35d)

34c

Well then, gentlemen, this is pretty much what I have to say in my defence – this and perhaps some other things of this sort. But perhaps one of you may resent it when he remembers his own case – how when he was on trial for lesser charges than these he begged and pleaded with the jurors, shed many a tear, and **had his children come in** together with many other family and friends, in order to produce as much pity as he could, while I will do none of this, even though I face what appears to be the ultimate danger. Perhaps someone thinking of this may

34d

harden his heart against me and angrily cast his vote against me. If any of you feels this way – I myself don't expect this, but just in case – I think it would be reasonable to tell him this.

'I do indeed, best of men, have a family. The line from Homer applies: I was not born *from oak or stone* but from human beings, so yes, I have a family, gentlemen of Athens, and sons, three of them, **one now a youth, two still young children**. But nevertheless I will not have them come up here, nor will I beg you to change your votes.'

34e

So why will I do none of this? Not out of stubbornness, gentlemen of Athens, nor out of disrespect for you. No, whether I am courageous in the face of death

---

had his children come in   this was such a standard practice in Athenian trials (as at Lysias 20.34) that Aristophanes spoofs it in his play, *Wasps* (976–9). There a pet dog is put on trial for stealing cheese, and the puppies are brought in and told to whimper to help save their father; their whimpers help win over the jury. Compare the modern practice of making sure the family of the defendant is seated prominently in the courtroom.

from oak or stone   a proverbial phrase which appears in *Odyssey* 19.163. In her interview with her husband, Odysseus, who is disguised as a beggar, Penelope attempts to get him to reveal who his parents are by noting that he can't have been born from oak or stone. Odysseus then tells her one of his false tales.

one now a youth, two still young children   Socrates had three sons, Lamprocles (born by 416), Sophroniscus (born by 410), and Menexenus (born by 402), none of whom has left much of a mark behind in the historical record.

or not is another story, but given my reputation it does not seem a fine thing for me, for you, or for the whole of the city for me to do anything of this sort, not at my age, not with the reputation that I have. It may be true or it may be false, but people have made up their minds that Socrates is in some way superior to most people. If those of you who are held to surpass others in wisdom or courage or any other virtue turn out to be the sort of people who would do such things, that would be shameful. Many times have I seen such people on trial, people who had appeared to amount to something but then went to amazing lengths, thinking that they would suffer something fearful if they died – as if they would be immortal if you didn't kill them. They seem to me to have covered the city with shame, so that anyone from out of town would assume that Athenians who were outstanding in virtue, who were selected for office or other honours, were **no better than women**. I say this, gentlemen of Athens, because you shouldn't do this, those of you who are thought to amount to anything at all, nor, if I try to do it, should you allow me. Instead this is what you should show: you are far more ready to condemn one who produces all this pitiful drama and makes the city fit for mockery than one who keeps his peace.

35a

35b

no better than women   with remarks like these Socrates appears to endorse the dominant view of women in fifth-century Athens. In this view women were physically, intellectually, and morally inferior to men. Rather similarly, Plato will report that Socrates sent his wife Xanthippe away when it was time for him to drink the hemlock, and will have Socrates chide his (male) friends for crying like women (*Phaedo* 60a–b, 116b, 117d–e). On the other hand, at **41c** (p. 79) Socrates will imagine himself talking not only with men but with women in the afterlife, though this may simply be in keeping with mythological precedents (see the note there). Socrates elsewhere says that he had two women teachers, Diotima, a (perhaps fictional) priestess from the Greek city of Mantinea (Plato, *Symposium* 201d–212c), and **Aspasia**, Pericles' controversial partner (Plato, *Menexenus* 235e–236d). Xenophon's Socrates also refers favourably to Aspasia (*Memorabilia* 2.6.36, *Oeconomicus* 3.14).

In the *Republic* (5.455c–456c), though it is a later work that may reflect Plato's views more than Socrates' (see pp. 4–6 for more on this aspect of what is called **The Socratic Question**), Plato will have Socrates argue that the souls of women have the same sort of potential as do those of men, even if the average woman has less of this potential than the average man does. Women should therefore be educated in the same way as men and, in exceptional cases, should be allowed to rule. Probably Socrates, like most men of pre-modern times, even the most thoughtful and observant among them, did not allow his recognition that a few women were his equal to undermine his inherited belief that most men were superior to most women. As precious few Greek women were given an education, Greek sexism reinforced itself circularly: women were held to be inferior to men, and so received an inferior education, which meant that Greek women did appear intellectually inferior to Greek men.

35c Even apart from reputation, gentlemen, justice appears to me to demand not that I beg the jury or escape punishment by begging, but rather that I inform and persuade the jury. For a juror does not sit in order to render a corrupt judgement, but to decide what is just. He has not **taken an oath** to do a favour to whomever he chooses to favour, but to give a verdict in accordance with the laws. Therefore I must not get you into the habit of committing perjury, nor should you get into that habit yourselves – for then neither of us would be pious. So do not think, gentlemen of the jury, that I should treat you in a way that I believe to be neither

35d admirable nor pious, especially given that I am, by Zeus, being charged with impiety by Meletus over here. For if by my begging I tried to persuade and force you to ignore your oath, I would be teaching you to believe that the gods do not exist, and in the very act of defending myself I would actually be accusing myself of not recognizing the gods. That's far from being the case. For I do recognize them, gentlemen of Athens, as none of my accusers does, and I leave it to you and to the god to judge my case as will turn out best both for me and for you.

1 So why won't Socrates resort to begging the jury to let him off?

2 Would you have your friends and family appear in court to support you if you were on trial for your life?

3 If you had managed to avoid being convicted of a crime by begging for mercy, would what Socrates says here make you more or less inclined to convict him?

4 Socrates says here that most people think he is in some way superior. Does this contradict what he says about his reputation elsewhere in this speech?

5 Would you choose to die for your principles even if it meant leaving behind young children who depended on you?

The juror's oath

We can piece together the oath sworn by Athenian jurors from a number of places where it is mentioned in other speeches. Here's more or less how it went:

I will cast my vote in accordance with the laws and the decrees of the Assembly of Athens and of the Council of 500, and, in matters where there is no law, I will vote in accordance with what I think is most just, and neither out of favouritism nor out of hatred. And I will vote only on the matters on trial, and will listen in the same way to both accusers and defendants alike. I swear by Zeus, by Apollo, and by Demeter, and if I keep my oath may I have much good fortune, but if I perjure myself may I and my family be destroyed.

taken an oath see the text box above. As the oath was sworn by the gods, breaking it would be impious.

Put yourself in the position of an Athenian juror who swore that oath in 399 BC. Five years ago Athens lost a war, her empire, and then, for a year, her democracy (to the Thirty Tyrants). You no doubt have lost friends in all of this, may well have lost family members, and you are almost certainly poorer than you were when the war began. Socrates was associated with the worst of the Thirty Tyrants, Critias, and with the most controversial other figure in Athens during the last years of that war, Alcibiades. And he clearly had at least some strange ideas about religion, as all this talk of his 'divine sign' makes clear enough. There's a law against impiety, probably a very vague law that you must interpret for yourself. Are you convinced by Socrates' defence?

Here's another role to play, and another way to think about the *Apology*. We've lost the prosecution speeches. What would the prosecutors have said? How could they have pre-empted Socrates' arguments? Write your own prosecution speech, and see how many people you can convince to convict Socrates. Good luck doing as well as Meletus and company did!

The penalty phase and the examined life (35e–38b)

35e I am not upset, gentlemen of Athens, at what has happened, **your vote to condemn**
36a **me.** There are many reasons for this, among them the fact that what happened came as no surprise. Actually, I am quite amazed at how the vote has come out, because I didn't think that the margin would be so small; I expected it would be far greater. As it turns out, it appears that if just thirty votes had gone the other way, I would have been acquitted. In fact, so far as Meletus is concerned, I think that even now I have been acquitted, and not only that: it is clear to everyone that if Anytus and Lycon hadn't come forward to accuse me, Meletus would actually
36b have owed a 1,000 drachma fine because **he didn't receive a fifth of the votes.**

---

your vote to condemn me Socrates has been found guilty by a vote of 280 to 220. The law against impiety did not specify a punishment. In such cases jurors were required to choose either the penalty sought by the prosecution (death in Socrates' case) or one suggested by the defendant.

he didn't receive a fifth of the votes as a way of discouraging frivolous prosecutions, Athenian law mandated that a prosecutor who didn't receive at least one-fifth of the votes was to pay a substantial fine of 1,000 drachmas. Socrates assumes that each speaker was responsible for one-third of the prosecution's 280 votes; that would leave Meletus with less than the 100 votes he'd need to escape a fine. Perhaps Socrates is relying on the fact that Meletus was a young man with far less influence than Anytus – or perhaps Socrates' mathematics is just a bit of gallows humour.

Well, this man thinks I deserve death as my penalty. So what penalty do I propose to you instead, gentlemen of Athens? Clearly one I deserve. What is that? What should happen to me, what fine should I pay because I did not keep to myself during my life, though I neglected the things most people are concerned with – making money through trade or running an estate, or becoming one of the generals or prominent public speakers or other office holders, or taking part in one of the political cliques or factions that rise up in the city – since I believed that

36c I really was too decent a person to escape with my life if I did such things? I did not pursue these things, where I would have been of no use either to you or to myself, but instead went to each of you in private, doing you the greatest service, I maintain, as I tried to persuade each of you not to take care of his possessions until he had taken care that he himself was as good and as thoughtful as he could be, and not to take care of **the city's possessions** before taking care of the city

36d herself, and to care for other things in the same way.

So what ought to happen to me for being this sort of man? Something good, gentlemen of Athens, at least if I am to get the punishment I truly deserve, and something good that suits me. So what would be appropriate for a poor benefactor who needs leisure in order to urge you on in this way? Nothing would be more appropriate for such a man, gentlemen of Athens, than **meals in the Prytaneum**. That's far more appropriate for him than for any of you who has won in the horse race, or the two- or four-horse chariot races at Olympia. For while that man makes

36e you *seem* happy, I make you *be* happy, and while **he has no need of this support**,

37a I do need it. So if I must be punished with my just deserts, this is the penalty I propose: meals in the Prytaneum.

Now perhaps in saying this I may appear every bit as stubborn as when I spoke about begging for mercy. But actually this isn't the case, gentlemen of Athens. It's more like this: I am persuaded that I have willingly done injustice to no man;

---

the city's possessions   Socrates probably means 'harbours and shipyards and walls and tribute and that sort of nonsense', as he puts it when describing the concerns of Athenian leaders at *Gorgias* **519a** (quoted on p. 14). If taking care of oneself means making oneself virtuous and thoughtful, what would taking care of the city itself mean?

meals in the Prytaneum   the Athenians honoured Olympic victors, distinguished generals, and the descendants of a few famous Athenians with daily meals in the Prytaneum, a public building that housed the communal hearth of the city and was regarded as its symbolic centre. Ambassadors to Athens and Athenian ambassadors back from a successful mission abroad were also invited. Socrates is thus suggesting not only that he be given free meals, but that he have a place of honour at official banquets.

he has no need of this support   it was the man (or, very rarely, the woman) who owned the horse or chariot and team of horses who was the Olympic victor, not the driver; as horses and chariots were expensive, victors in such events had to be wealthy.

but I'm failing to persuade you of this, because we have spoken together for only a short time. I think that if you had a law like other people do that **capital cases require not one day alone but many days**, you would have been convinced. As it is, it's no easy thing to refute such great slanders in such a short time.

As I'm convinced that I have never treated anyone unjustly, there's no way I will treat myself unjustly and attack myself by saying that I deserve some harm and assigning myself a harmful penalty. What am I to be afraid of? That I would suffer the penalty Meletus is proposing, when I maintain that I don't know whether it is something good or bad? Or am I instead to choose something that I'm sure is bad for me by proposing it as my punishment? Prison? But why should I live in jail, **enslaved to the successive sets of officers there, the eleven**? Or a fine instead, and be locked up until I can pay it? Well, that's exactly what I was saying just now – I don't have any money to pay it off. Or am I to be punished with exile? You may indeed perhaps punish me with this. But I'd really have to be in love with life, gentlemen of Athens, to be so foolish as to think that while you, my fellow citizens, weren't able to tolerate the arguments I spend my time on, arguments that became so burdensome and hateful to you that you now seek to free yourselves from them, other people will nevertheless turn out to be more tolerant. That will hardly be the case, gentlemen of Athens. So it's a fine life I'd live in exile at my age, exchanging one city for another as I'm driven out from each one of them in turn. For I'm sure that wherever I go, the young will listen to what I say, just as they do here. And if I drive them away, they themselves **will persuade their elders to exile me**. But if I do not drive them off, then their fathers and relatives will drive me off for the sake of their children.

Perhaps someone may say, 'Socrates, can't you please just shut up and keep to yourself, so you can go off and live your life in exile?' Convincing some of you about this is the hardest thing of all. For if I say that doing this would amount to disobeying the god and that this is why it's impossible for me to keep to myself,

37b

37c

37d

37e

38a

---

capital cases require not one day alone but many days Sparta was a prominent example of a city that did not resolve capital cases in a single day – and the pro-Spartan implication here could not have pleased the jury.

enslaved to the successive sets of officers there, the eleven each year eleven citizens were selected by lottery (as were most public officials in Athens) to supervise the jail and tend to other matters of public order. Socrates' point is that being a prisoner is equivalent to being a slave, and he wants nothing of it.

will persuade their elders to exile me Socrates rather fancifully imagines that young men would be so eager to speak with him that they would exile him for turning them away.

you won't believe me, since you'll think **I'm being ironic**. On the other hand, if I say that it so happens that the greatest good for a human being is to speak about virtue each day and about the other things you've heard me in conversation about, examining both myself and others, and that **a human life without examination is not worth living**, you'll believe me still less when I say this. But this is how it is, as I maintain, gentlemen, though it's not easy to convince you.

38b   Now I'm also not in the habit of thinking that I deserve some harm. If I were wealthy, I'd assign as my penalty all the money I could be expected to pay; that wouldn't harm me at all. As it is, this won't work, unless you are willing to make my punishment what little money I can pay. I could perhaps pay **a mina of silver**, more or less. So that's the penalty I suggest.

I'm being ironic Greek *eirōneia* was normally deceptive, so Socrates is saying that the jury will think he is merely pretending to be a humble and dutiful servant of the god, when what he is really doing is displaying his skill in argument by humiliating everyone he talks to. Socrates suggests, in other words, that the jury won't believe his tale about the oracle, or at least won't believe in the divine mission he has developed from that tale. In Plato's *Republic* (1.337a), Thrasymachus similarly attacks Socrates for pretending that he has no answer to the question at hand so that he can instead refute the answers others put forward. But **Socratic irony** can be more subtle: see p. 7 in chapter 1.

a human life without examination is not worth living this famous phrase, more often translated as 'the unexamined life is not worth living', sums up Socrates' philosophy as well as any few words can. My translation differs from the traditional one because the Greek doesn't only mean that you should submit your own life to examination: examining the lives of others counts too – and it is this that Socrates spends most of his time doing. Examining someone else's life also reflects on your own life, because our lives have more in common than not. For Socrates does not mean that *any* examined life is of equal value, that you can live however you choose, so long as you think through what you're doing; he seems to assume that there is *one best sort of life* for a human being, and that we should be able to agree about what that best life consists of. The best life that Socrates has managed to discover, as it turns out, is precisely the life spent in this sort of examination, rather than, say, a life of action. Hence when Socrates imagines an ideal afterlife (**41b** on p. 79), it is one spent in examination of heroes from Greek myth. For Socrates, then, inquiry into the best sort of life – the Socratic practice of philosophy – appears to be not only a means but an end. This may explain why Socrates notes that such a life is the best *human* one; the gods, unlike we humans, possess true wisdom, and hence for them a life spent in pursuit of wisdom would be meaningless.

a mina of silver as noted at **20b** (p. 36) above, a mina was worth 100 drachmas, and a drachma was one day's pay for a skilled worker. Xenophon (*Oeconomicus* 2.3) has Socrates report that his property, including his home, was worth five minas; if Xenophon was right, a one-mina fine would not have ruined Socrates, making it somewhat surprising that he offers only one mina. Perhaps one mina was all his ready cash, and he thus implicitly admits that a larger fine would harm him. But it is at least as likely that Plato and Xenophon were just thinking in broad terms of a relatively impoverished man who could not afford to pay a substantial fine. The 30-mina fine Socrates eventually agrees to pay, with help from his friends, was a substantial sum.

But **Plato here, gentlemen of Athens, and Crito and Critobulus and Apollodorus** are telling me to set the penalty at 30 minas, and that they will themselves guarantee payment. So I propose a penalty of that much, and they will be reliable guarantors to you for that amount of silver.

1 Why does Socrates believe that the unexamined life is not worth living, and that the life spent discussing virtue is the best life?

2 Socrates thinks that many jurors will doubt his claim to be on a divine mission, and that even fewer will believe him when he says that only the examined life is worth living. Why is he so sure that they won't believe him? Do you believe him?

3 On the other hand, Socrates says that if he had had more time to speak with the jury, he could have convinced them of the truth of what he says. What could he have said to convince them?

4 A late and perhaps unreliable source (Diogenes Laertius 2.42) tells us that in the sentencing phase Socrates lost an additional 80 votes, so that while Socrates was first found guilty by a vote of 280 to 220, the vote for death in the sentencing phase was 360 to 140. Reread this section as if you were a juror who had voted to acquit Socrates, but now had to assign a punishment to him. Can you see why some jurors who had originally voted to acquit Socrates were so angered by what he said here that they voted for death?

Socrates the mystic

This late antique bust of Socrates, presumably based on an idealizing **type B** portrait, departs still further from the idea that Socrates resembled a **satyr**. It is Socrates' eyes that strike us here – and not because they bulge out, as our earliest sources have it, but because of the enraptured look they lend the bust, a look accentuated by the open mouth. Socrates, as other intellectuals in late antiquity, was given a mystical makeover to allow him to serve as a spiritual guide for the very different world of the third and fourth centuries AD, when pagans vied with Christians for popular support. Socrates' gaze no longer engages the viewer, but looks off to some distant, transcendent truth.

Socrates, bust from Ephesus, c. AD 300.

- In late antiquity, pagans fighting off Christians enlisted Socrates as an ally. What groups would want to associate themselves with Socrates today? And what would they want him to look like in order to best advance their cause?

Plato here, gentlemen of Athens, and Crito and Critobulus and Apollodorus for these individuals, see the notes at **33e–34a** on pp. 66–7.

Socrates' final speech (38c–42a)

The jury has now condemned Socrates to death. Yet Socrates manages one last speech. There is no precedent for this sort of extra speech in our evidence for Athenian legal procedures, and it is hard to imagine that jurors who had just condemned Socrates would not make an uproar if he went on like this. So this part of the *Apology* is probably fictional, although what Socrates says could be based on remarks he made after the trial. Compare modern courtroom dramas – even those 'based on a true story' – in which characters make stirring speeches that no judge (much less opposing legal counsel) would have allowed to take place during an actual trial.

38c **You haven't gained much time**, gentlemen of Athens, and you'll win a name for being to blame, in the eyes of those who want to criticize the city, for killing Socrates, a wise man – and they will indeed maintain that I am wise, even if I am not, they who wish to reproach you. For if you had waited a short time, this would have happened without your doing anything. You see how far along I've

38d come in life, how near I am to death. I say this not to all of you, but to those who condemned me to death, and to the same people I would also add this: you perhaps believe, gentlemen, that I've been convicted because I was at a loss for words, the words that would have convinced you, had I believed that I should do and say whatever it took to escape this verdict. Far from it. I was indeed convicted because I lacked something: I was not boldfaced and shameless enough to be willing to give you what would have given you the most pleasure to hear – me

38e grieving and crying and doing and saying many other things that I say are beneath me, the sorts of things you are accustomed to hear from others. But I thought then that I must not do anything **slavish** because of the danger, nor do I think otherwise now, after I've made this defence. No, I prefer by far to make this sort of defence and die than to make that sort and live.

You haven't gained much time   by killing the 70-year-old Socrates, who would have died soon enough naturally.

slavish   in a society in which slavery was omnipresent (as many as one-third of the people living in ancient Athens were slaves) and was largely taken for granted, discussion of slavery was centred not on the justice of the institution but on how a legally free man should act in a *morally* free way. A slave is, by legal definition, a man not in control of himself; and a free man who lacked self-control was therefore thought to be slavish. Socrates argues that his refusal to stoop to begging for his life shows that he is – unlike most Athenians in his position – a truly free man, one who can control any inclination to plead for his life and can therefore stick to his principles. Compare the discussion Socrates and **Aristippus** have about living slavishly in Xenophon, *Memorabilia* **2.1.9–19** (pp. 111–15), and what Callicles says about slavish men in Plato's *Gorgias* **483b** (p. 140); a note to the second passage discusses an ancient defence of slavery.

39a   Neither in court nor in war should I or anyone else try to do whatever it takes to escape death. In battle, too, it's often clear that you can escape death by abandoning your arms and begging the enemy for mercy. There are many other ways to escape death in every sort of danger, if you are boldfaced enough to do and say whatever it takes. No, it's not this that is difficult, gentlemen, escaping

39b   death; it is far harder to escape becoming a poor excuse for a man, a condition which outruns death. So now I, slow and old as I am, was caught by the slower thing, while my accusers, who are cunning and swift, were caught by the swifter pursuer, wickedness. So now I will depart, condemned by you to death, while truth has condemned these men of being vile and unjust. I stand by my judgement of them, as they stand by their judgement of me. Perhaps things had to turn out like this, and I believe this will do well enough.

39c   Next I want to deliver a prophecy to you who have condemned me, as I have reached the point at which people are most prophetic, **as they are about to die**. I maintain, gentlemen, you who have killed me, that punishment will come to you soon after my death, a punishment far more difficult, by Zeus, than that you have inflicted by killing me. You acted out of the belief that you would escape from having your lives examined. But the result for you will be quite the opposite, as

39d   I maintain. There will be **more people around to examine you**, people I've been holding in check for now, though you did not realize it. And they will be more difficult to handle, as they are younger, and you will resent them more. If you believe that by killing people you can avoid having people reproach you with not living the right way, you're not reasoning very well. Your escape attempt probably won't succeed, and it is hardly admirable. But there is another way that is both most admirable and easy: rather than punishing others who would examine you, make yourself the best that you can be.

With this, then, I am done prophesying to those who have condemned me.

39e   But I'd enjoy speaking with those who have voted to acquit me about what's happened, **while the officials are busy** and I am not yet going off to where I must die. Just stay with me, gentlemen, for this short time, since nothing prevents us

---

as they are about to die   there was (and is) a widespread belief that those on the point of death can see into the future, perhaps because as the soul is freed from the body it can see more clearly.

more people around to examine you   Plato thus alludes to his own role, together with the other followers of Socrates. Eventually there were stories of a backlash against the prosecutors; but see the footnote to **18b** (p. 32).

while the officials are busy   presumably we are to imagine them making arrangements for Socrates' transfer to prison. It appears that Socrates here speaks informally with friendly jurors as the rest of the jury is leaving the court, but he seems to address the whole jury again at the very end of his speech.

40a from chatting with each other for as long as it's possible to do so. I am ready to explain to you, as friends, the meaning of what has happened to me just now.

Gentlemen of the jury – for **you may correctly be called jurors** – something amazing has happened to me. The prophecy that often comes to me, **the daimonic one**, always came quite frequently in the past, opposing me even in quite small things if I was about to make a mistake. And you yourselves can see what has happened to me just now; it's something one could consider the worst

40b of evils, and indeed it is thought to be such. But the sign of the god opposed me neither when I left home this morning nor when I came here to court, nor as I was about to say anything at any point during my speech. On other occasions it often stopped me in the midst of saying something. Yet it did not oppose me about any thing I've done or said today. So how do I explain this? I'll tell you. Probably what has happened to me has been a good thing, and there's no way we could be

40c correct to understand it otherwise, those of us who think that death is an evil. For there's no way that my customary sign would have failed to oppose me if I weren't about to benefit.

Let us consider another reason to be very hopeful that death is something good. Death is one of two things. Either it is like not existing at all, and the dead do not feel anything; or, as some say, death is a transformation and transfer of the soul from here to another place. Now if there is no sensation, but death is like sleeping

40d without having any dreams at all, death would be an amazing gain. For I believe that if anyone picked that one night in which he slept so deeply that he saw no dreams, compared the other nights and days of his life with that night, and then considered the matter and told us how many of the days and nights in his life

40e were better and more pleasant than this one, he would find precious few of them – and that goes not only for just anyone, but even for the **Great King**. So if death is something of this sort, I say that it's a gain. For in this case eternity seems to me no longer than a single night.

But if to die is to emigrate, as it were, from here to another place, and what some say about it is true, that all the dead really do exist there, what greater good could

41a there be, gentlemen of the jury? If one reaches Hades, escapes those who claim

---

you may correctly be called jurors   up to this point, Socrates has regularly addressed the jurors only as Athenians, not as jurors. In Greek, a juror (*dikastēs*) is one who renders justice (*dikē*), and in Socrates' view only those who voted to acquit him have done so.

the daimonic one   see **31d–e** (pp. 61–2).

Great King   the king of Persia, as the richest and most powerful man known to most Greeks, was sometimes considered the paragon of happiness. But Greek writers also often note that the happiness of those in power could be fleeting, and the riches and power of the king may make him a strange example for the poor and powerless Socrates to put forward.

to be **judges** here, and finds those who are true judges, the ones said to give judgements there, **Minos and Rhadamanthus and Aeacus and Triptolemus** and the other heroes who proved just during their lives, would that be a worthless move? And what wouldn't you be willing to give to meet **Orpheus and Musaeus and Hesiod and Homer**?

41b If this is true, I am ready to die many times over. For it would be amazing to spend my time there, to meet **Palamedes and Ajax, son of Telamon**, and any other of the men of old who died through an unjust verdict, and compare my experiences with theirs. I don't believe this would be unpleasant, and the greatest thing would be to go on examining and investigating as I do here, to see who of them is wise and who thinks he is, but isn't. What wouldn't one be willing to

41c give, gentlemen of the jury, to examine **the man who led the huge army** against Troy, or **Odysseus or Sisyphus** or the countless other men and **women** one could name? It would be almost too much happiness to speak with them and meet them and examine them. At any rate, they certainly don't kill people there for doing this. People there are better off than people here in many respects, and especially because they are immortal from this time forward, if what is said is indeed true.

---

judges   the same Greek word (*dikastes*) is translated as 'juror' elsewhere; recall that the Athenians had no judges apart from the many citizens serving as jurors. But 'judges' works better here, as the mythological judicial system of the underworld reflects a pre-democratic state of affairs where a few leading men made the legal decisions.

Minos and Rhadamanthus and Aeacus and Triptolemus   the first three were sons of Zeus and were early kings, Minos and Rhadamanthus on Crete, Aeacus on the island of Aegina near Athens. Triptolemus, from Eleusis outside of Athens, was taught how to grow grain by the goddess Demeter, and, in Athenian myth, was responsible for sharing this lesson with all mankind.

Orpheus and Musaeus and Hesiod and Homer   were among the most respected Greek poets. Orpheus and Musaeus were figures of legend, and associated with mystery cults that promised a better afterlife. Hesiod and Homer were active around 700.

Palamedes and Ajax, son of Telamon   in Greek myth Palamedes was framed by Odysseus, who envied his wisdom. Ajax was driven mad when he was cheated of the arms of Achilles, again by Odysseus.

the man who led the huge army   Agamemnon, legendary king of Mycenae, and leader of the Greek army at Troy.

Odysseus or Sisyphus   Odysseus, hero of Homer's *Odyssey*, was known for his cunning. Sisyphus is the fellow who was punished by having to push the rock to the top of the hill, always to have it tumble back down; he too was cunning, cunning enough to cheat death, until the gods finally gave him his just deserts.

women   perhaps Socrates is thinking of the line-up of heroines Odysseus talks with in Homer's *Odyssey* (11.225–332). For Socrates' views on women, see the note at **35b** on p. 69.

41d And so, gentlemen of the jury, you ought to be of good hope regarding death and to keep this one truth in mind: **nothing can harm a good man**, whether living or dead, nor are his affairs neglected by the gods. What's happened to me is not due to chance; no, it is clear to me that at this point it was better for me to die and be done **with my troubles**. This is why the sign never turned me back, and I for my part am not terribly upset with those who voted against me or with my accusers. Of course they did not vote against me or accuse me thinking that I'd be better

41e off, but believed they would harm me. Here they deserve blame. But this is all I ask of them. Take your revenge, gentlemen, on my sons, when they come of age, and make them suffer exactly what I made you suffer, if they appear to you to be more concerned with money or anything else than with virtue. And if they think that they amount to something when they do not, reproach them as I did you, because they are not concerned with what they should be concerned with, and think they amount to something when they are in fact worthless. Do this and

42a you'll have treated me as is just, me and my sons.

But now it is time to depart, I to die, and you to live. Which of us goes to something better is unclear to all except to the god.

---

1 Earlier, Socrates argued that it was foolish to fear death, because no one knows what death will bring (**29a–b**, p. 56). But here he suggests further ways we can think about death. What explains the difference in approach? Does what he says here contradict what he said before?

2 If death is really such a good thing, is Socrates heroic in facing it bravely?

3 Socrates claims that death is either a dreamless sleep or, at least for him, a wonderful continuation of his life of questioning, now with an all-star cast from Greek myth. Isn't it odd that a man who described his mission as waking up the citizens of Athens (**30e**, p. 60) says here that an eternity of dreamless sleep would be a tremendous gain?

4 On the other hand, how can Socrates be so hopeful that the afterlife will consist of delightful philosophical conversations? It is far dimmer in Greek myth (see book 11 of Homer's *Odyssey*). Of course in some real sense Socrates' conversations do continue: witness your reading this book.

5 Does Socrates' prophecy at **39c–d** (p. 77) come true?

---

nothing can harm a good man   compare **30d** (p. 60), though there Socrates says only that a worse man cannot harm a better one.

with my troubles   probably those of old age, as Xenophon makes clear at the beginning of his *Apology*.

3 Plato's *Laches*

Introduction

The *Laches* is a discussion of courage, Greek *andreia*, a term closely connected to the Greek word for 'man' (*anēr*, pl. *andres*) and hence most literally translated as 'manliness'. The most traditional form of courage was that shown in battle, and it is therefore natural that Socrates' main conversation partners in this dialogue are two generals, Laches and Nicias, men who could be expected to be experts on this topic. Of course we expect that **Plato** will show Socrates besting these generals on the topic of courage, and he does.

Why show that these two generals in particular fail to understand courage? Neither was a coward in the most conventional sense: both fought courageously in many a battle. But both suffered from a more complex failure of courage at the crucial moment in their careers. Laches attacked when over-eager soldiers convinced him and the other generals leading an allied army to abandon high ground and meet a Spartan army on the plains at Mantinea. The resulting battle was a Spartan victory, in which Laches himself died (see the note at **193a** on p. 90). Nicias, on the other hand, failed to retreat when he should have, because the seers accompanying the army warned that the signs were not right for such a move. The result was the disastrous end of the Athenian expedition in Sicily: many thousands of Athenians died, including Nicias himself, who was murdered after being taken captive (see the text box on pp. 105–6). Thus Laches was arguably not courageous enough to stay put rather than attack, and Nicias was not courageous enough to retreat rather than stay put: courage is more complicated than we may have thought.

The dialogue opens with two close friends, the elderly gentlemen Lysimachus and Melesias, seeking advice about how to educate their sons. The two have taken their sons to see an expert trainer of **hoplites**, the heavily armed infantrymen who were the most important part of classical Greek armies. They have brought along our two generals as advisers, but the generals disagree on the value of the specialized training offered by the expert (see p. 86), and Socrates is called upon to mediate. Our excerpts from the dialogue begin as Socrates redirects the conversation to consideration of the nature of courage. When it becomes clear that neither he nor either of the generals can name an expert teacher he's had on the topic, and that none of them can point to cases where they've led men to become courageous, Socrates suggests another approach: the attempt to define courage.

Socrates rescues Alcibiades

Marble relief by Antonio Canova, 1797.

The Italian neoclassical sculptor Antonio Canova produced a series of reliefs of Socrates, most depicting the familiar scenes of Socrates' trial and death. This one shows a scene much rarer in art, the philosopher (the bearded figure on the left) rescuing a wounded **Alcibiades** outside Potidaea in 430 BC (described in Plato, *Symposium*, **220d–e**, quoted on the next page). Canova apparently found Socrates' bravery personally appealing; the Socrates reliefs seem to have been made for Canova's own personal enjoyment, rather than for a patron or for public display.

- What is Canova's representation of the physical features, stance, and relative positions of Alcibiades and Socrates meant to tell us about these two men and their relationship to one another?

Socrates in battle

In Plato's *Symposium*, Socrates' controversial associate Alcibiades relates Socrates' exploits in battle, first at a battle in 430, when the Spartans defeated an Athenian army making its way back to Athens after the successful siege of Potidaea, then at the battle of Delion in 424, where the Boeotians, allies of Sparta, had defeated the Athenians. Near the end of the sophisticated drinking party portrayed in Plato's *Symposium*, Alcibiades arrives, uninvited and drunk, and praises Socrates before the assembled guests, who include the comic poet **Aristophanes** and Socrates himself.

> And, if you'd like, also hear how he acted in battle, for it is only just to give him credit for this too. During the battle for which the generals gave me the **award of valour**, it was no one other than he who saved me. He was unwilling to leave me behind when I was wounded, but saved both me and my weapons. So I, Socrates, was telling the generals to give the award of valour to you – you won't criticize me here and say that I'm not telling the truth. In fact, when the generals wanted to give me the award, since the only thing they were taking into account was my status, you yourself wanted me to get it instead of you, and wanted this even more than the generals did.
>
> And, gentlemen, Socrates was also worth seeing when the army was withdrawing from Delion. I was there in the cavalry, while he was serving on foot. Our men had already scattered, and he was retreating alongside Laches. I met up with him, and when I saw him I told him to take heart and that I would not abandon him. I got a closer look at Socrates there than I had at Potidaea (I was less fearful this time, since I was on horseback). First, I saw how much more composed he was than Laches. Then indeed, Aristophanes, as you've put it, 'he was **swaggering and casting his eyes from side to side**', calmly looking over friends and foes alike so as to make it clear to all, even from far off, that anyone who attacked this man would have himself quite a fight. As a result, both he and his companion got away unhurt. For in war those who act like this are rarely attacked; it's those who turn and run who get chased down.
>
> (*Symposium* 220d–221c)

- None of the participants in the *Laches* bring up their own experiences in battle when discussing courage. But can we learn anything about Socrates' understanding of courage from his behaviour in battle?

- What other examples of courageous behaviour by Socrates have you encountered so far? Is there something about Socrates' pursuit of philosophy that made him braver than most people?

---

award of valour   after a major battle the generals in command would award a wreath and set of armour to the soldier deemed to have fought most valiantly.

swaggering and casting his eyes from side to side   an adaptation of Aristophanes, *Clouds* 362.

Courage as remaining at one's post (Plato, *Laches* 189e–192b)

189e   SOCRATES   If we know that the presence of one thing makes something else better, and are also able to make the first thing present in the second, then we clearly understand the first thing, and could be asked to provide advice about the best way to acquire it easily. Now **perhaps you don't understand what I mean**, but will understand it

190a   more readily like this. If, for example, we knew that the presence of sight makes eyes better, and we were able to produce sight in eyes, clearly we would understand what sight is. And it's sight we were being asked about, asked how one can best and most easily acquire it. For if we didn't understand this very thing, what sight is, or what hearing is, we'd hardly be valuable advisers or doctors about eyes or

190b   ears – about the best way of acquiring hearing or sight.

     LACHES   You're right, Socrates.

     SOCRATES   Well, Laches, aren't these two men asking for our advice about how to produce **virtue** in the **souls** of their sons and make them better?

     LACHES   Certainly.

     SOCRATES   So don't we have to start out with this, understanding just what virtue is? For **if we didn't have any idea at all of what virtue is, how**

190c   **would we advise anyone about how best to acquire it?**

     LACHES   I don't think there's any way to do that, Socrates.

     SOCRATES   So we maintain, Laches, that we do know what it is.

     LACHES   Yes, we do.

     SOCRATES   And if we understand something, surely we could also say what it is.

     LACHES   Certainly.

     SOCRATES   Well, my good man, let's not investigate the whole of virtue right away, as that would perhaps be too large a task. But let's first see if we are in a position to understand some part of it adequately. This

190d   will probably make the investigation easier for us.

---

perhaps you don't understand what I mean Socrates' language is confusing because he is both introducing and attempting to defend a methodological principle modern scholars call the Priority of Definition. In order to know whether someone is courageous, for example, or to advise anyone on how to become courageous, we must first be able to define courage.

if we didn't have any idea at all of what virtue is, how would we advise anyone about how best to acquire it taken to an extreme, the principle of the Priority of Definition (see the prior note) results in something called 'the Socratic fallacy', the belief that to know *anything* about some trait, we must be able to define it first. In its extreme form this 'fallacy' is self-defeating: to know anything about a given trait one must first know *everything* about it. The version Socrates provides here is more commonsensical, even banal: to understand how to acquire virtue one must know *something* about virtue. But that something will turn out to be an understanding of the relevant virtue, courage, which will prove beyond the reach of the characters in this dialogue.

LACHES	Yes, Socrates, let's do as you wish.
SOCRATES	Now **which of the parts of virtue** should we choose? Or isn't it clear that it's the goal we aim at when learning how to fight in armour? And no doubt most people take that goal to be courage. Right?
LACHES	They do indeed.
SOCRATES	So let's first attempt, Laches, to say what courage is. After that we will investigate how the young can acquire it, **insofar as it can be acquired through training and learning**. Well, try to answer my question: what is courage?
LACHES	By Zeus, Socrates, that's not hard to say. If someone is willing **to stay in the battle line** and fight off the enemy and not flee, you can be sure that he is courageous.
SOCRATES	That's well said, Laches; but perhaps my failure to speak clearly is to blame for your answering a question different from the one I intended to ask.
LACHES	What do you mean by this, Socrates?
SOCRATES	I'll explain as best I can. Surely this man you mention, he who stays in line and fights the enemy, is courageous.
LACHES	I'd certainly say so.
SOCRATES	So do I. But what about a man who fights the enemy as he flees, rather than holding his ground?
LACHES	How does one flee and fight?

190e (margin, beside "investigate how the young...")

191a (margin, beside "I'll explain as best I can...")

---

which of the parts of virtue   the assumption that virtue has distinct parts will play a major role later in the argument (**198a**, p. 103), though here it appears to be introduced simply to make things easier.

insofar as it can be acquired through training and learning   this little clause is rather important, as it hints at aspects of courage that are otherwise downplayed in the dialogue. Courage could be a quality that one is born with, or born without. In Socrates' day there was considerable argument about whether virtue (or excellence, the Greek *aretē*) could be taught, and this question is at the heart of two Platonic dialogues, the *Meno* and the *Protagoras*. In traditional Greek thought, virtue ran in the best families (i.e., among the aristocracy), a view which conveniently reinforced the power of a few leading aristocratic clans. But influential aristocrats often had mediocre sons, which showed that inheritance wasn't everything; Lysimachus and Melesias, the fathers seeking Socrates' advice here about how to train their sons, are a case in point. They themselves were far less influential than their own fathers, and it was perhaps an awareness of this that led them to seek a better education for their sons. This sort of education was offered by the **sophists**, who claimed to teach virtue, if one could pay their fees – which conveniently enriched the sophists, and meant that only the rich could acquire virtue this way. We too wonder about how character is formed, of course, with some people emphasizing 'nature' (genes), others 'nurture' (education in school, by parents, or by peers). Which do you think is more important?

to stay in the battle line   compare what Socrates says at *Apology* **28d** on p. 55.

Hoplites in action

The Chigi Vase, c. 640 BC.

This vase has played a large role in a modern debate about how Greeks fought, a debate relevant to the issues raised in the *Laches*. In one view, hoplites fought in a phalanx formation that was so tightly packed that individual skill would have made little difference. This image seems to show such a formation, but the soldiers are in fact hoisting throwing spears, so must be imagined to be some distance apart. The compressed appearance of the formation does not so much reflect the realities of the battlefield as the constraints of the narrow field available on the vase. Thus the skills offered by the expert trainer who is discussed at the outset of the *Laches* (before our excerpts from the dialogue begin) would have had real value. But the ancient idealization of the virtuous citizen-soldier made such specialized training controversial, and hence it is no surprise that the two generals of our dialogue could not agree on whether or not it was valuable for young men. As the trainer offered a new form of special expertise in warfare, the sophists offered new-fangled expertise in peaceful pursuits. Socrates agreed with these controversial experts that expertise was needed, but had his own ideas about what sort of knowledge was required.

- What counts more for us, courage or skill? And are there other areas of life where we are more interested in a person's character than in their expertise?

	SOCRATES	Well, I suppose it's like what the **Scythians** are said to do, to fight no less in flight than in pursuit. And **Homer**, of course, praises the horses of Aeneas, saying that they *knew how to rush this way and that both in pursuit and in flight.* And because of this he praised Aeneas for his understanding of fear, and said that he was a *master of fright.*
191b		
	LACHES	That's well and good, Socrates, since he was talking about chariots. And you're talking about Scythian horsemen. Cavalry fights like that, but hoplites fight as I've described them.
191c	SOCRATES	Except, perhaps, for the Spartans, Laches. For people say that at **Plataea**, when they approached the men with the wicker shields, the Spartans were unwilling to stay and fight against them, but fled, and when the ranks of the Persians got confused, the Spartans turned on them, fought them like cavalry, and thus won the battle there.
	LACHES	You're right.
191d	SOCRATES	Well, this is why I was saying just now that it was my asking a poor question that was to blame for your giving a poor answer. For I wanted to learn from you not only who is courageous fighting as a hoplite, but who is courageous while fighting on horseback and in warfare in general, and not only in war, but also who is courageous in the presence of the dangers at sea, who is courageous about sickness, and who courageous about poverty or about **the risks of political life**; furthermore, I wanted to learn not only who is courageous about pain

---

Scythians a nomadic people based in what is now Ukraine. Superior horsemen, they often frustrated their foes by refusing to stand and fight, preferring to harass them from horseback. See Herodotus 4.1–144, especially 4.46.

Homer Socrates quotes loosely from *Iliad* 8.106–8. The speaker, the Greek hero Diomedes, has captured horses that had belonged to the Trojan Aeneas; he praises them while offering a ride to another Greek, Nestor, whose own chariot was disabled during a Greek retreat. Socrates playfully distorts the description of Aeneas, which refers to Aeneas' instilling fear in others, not to his willingness to give in to fear himself; Laches will ignore Socrates' joke about Aeneas. But the heroes of Homer's *Iliad* do not regularly fight in regular formations like the hoplites of Socrates' day did; Homeric battles are often free-flowing affairs in which both vigorous pursuit and timely flight have their place.

Plataea was the great Greek victory over the invading land forces of the Persians during the Persian wars (479 BC). Plato may be alluding to the Spartan technique of luring enemies forward with mock retreats, though this manoeuvre is not otherwise attested for the battle of Plataea, for which our best account comes in the work of the historian Herodotus (9.25–89). The 'men with wicker shields' are the infantry of the Persians; Herodotus says that the Persians fought as courageously as the Spartans, but lost because they were less skilled and were not as well armed (9.62–3).

the risks of political life those active in politics at Athens risked heavy fines or exile, which were common penalties for poor performance. Compare *Apology* **31d–32a** on pp. 61–2.

191e

or fear, but who is **good at battling against desire or pleasure**, either by staying put or turning back. For there surely are some, Laches, who are courageous in such things too.

LACHES   Very much so, Socrates.

SOCRATES   So all of these people are courageous; some are courageous in the presence of pleasures, others in the presence of pains, some in the presence of desires, and others in the presence of fears, while others, I believe, are cowardly in the presence of these same things.

LACHES   Of course.

SOCRATES   So just what is the courage shown in each of these cases? That's what I was asking about. Try again, first of all, to say what single thing courage is in all of these situations. Or do you not yet understand what I mean?

LACHES   Not quite.

192a

SOCRATES   Well, it's like this. If I were asking what quickness is, the quickness we may have both in running and in playing a lyre and in speaking and in learning and in many other things – if we have it to any degree, it's either in things done with our hands or our legs, or in speaking with our mouths, or in thought. Isn't this what you say?

LACHES   Of course.

SOCRATES   Well, if someone were to ask me, 'Socrates, what is this thing which you term quickness in all these areas?', I would tell him this: 'I call quickness the ability to accomplish many things in a short time, whether in speaking or racing or anything else.'

192b

LACHES   And you'd be correct to say that.

SOCRATES   So you too try, Laches, to explain courage in this same way. What single ability is found both in the presence of pleasure and pain and in all the cases we said it occurred in just now, and is therefore called courage?

---

1   How does Socrates manage to transform a debate about whether training in fighting in armour is a good idea to a quest for the meaning of courage?

2   Do you have to know how to define courage in order to advise a young man whether or not to get military training?

3   Just what is wrong with Laches' statement that courage consists in holding one's ground in battle?

4   Does it really take courage to battle against desires and pleasures? Or is that another sort of character trait altogether?

5   How much alike are courage and quickness? We can do pretty much anything quickly or slowly. Can we do everything in a courageous or cowardly way?

6   Try to answer Socrates' question: what single trait is present in any action you would call 'courageous'?

---

good at battling against desire or pleasure   as the last few words in this sentence reveal, Socrates was aware that such cases are not routinely considered examples of courage in his day (or ours). In Greek terms, resistance to pleasure and desire would more often be credited to the virtue of moderation (Greek *sōphrosynē*).

Courage as prudent endurance (192b–194b)

192c   LACHES   Well, courage seems to me to be a certain endurance of the soul, if one must name the disposition common to all these cases.

SOCRATES   Surely that's what we must do, if we are to answer our question. But this is how it looks to me: it isn't just any sort of endurance that looks like courage to you, I believe. Here's what I'm going on. I'm pretty sure, Laches, that you consider courage to be a very admirable thing.

LACHES   You can be sure that I consider it to be one of the most admirable things.

SOCRATES   Now is endurance **admirable and good** when it is prudent?

LACHES   Of course.

192d   SOCRATES   What about endurance when it isn't prudent? Isn't it the opposite of that, harmful and vicious?

LACHES   Yes.

SOCRATES   Now will you say that something of this sort, something vicious and harmful, is admirable?

LACHES   That wouldn't be right, Socrates.

SOCRATES   So you won't agree that this sort of endurance is courage, since it isn't admirable, and courage is an admirable thing.

LACHES   You're right.

SOCRATES   So by your argument courage will be *prudent* endurance.

LACHES   Probably so.

192e   SOCRATES   Let's consider what it is prudent about. Is it about everything large and small? For example, if someone endures in spending money prudently, knowing that by spending he will acquire more, would you call him courageous?

LACHES   I would not, by Zeus.

SOCRATES   Well, what if there's a doctor, and his son or someone else suffers pneumonia and begs his father **to let him drink or eat**, and he doesn't

193a   yield but endures and tells him no?

LACHES   No, that's not it at all.

SOCRATES   Well, what if a man prudently calculates and endures and is willing to fight, because he knows that others will come to his aid, that he

---

admirable and good   for the meaning of this phrase, see the note at *Apology* **20b**, p. 36.

to let him drink or eat   ancient doctors believed that diet was a crucial part not only of preventing but of curing disease. Some evidently believed that fasting helped in cases of pneumonia.

---

		is fighting against fewer men and worse ones than those on his side, and that he **holds the better position**? Would you say that a man who endures with the aid of this sort of prudent preparation is more courageous than the man in the opposing army who is willing to hold his ground and endure the fight?
193b	LACHES	The **man in the opposing army** seems more courageous to me, Socrates.
	SOCRATES	And yet his endurance is less prudent than that of the other man.
	LACHES	You're right.
	SOCRATES	So you will also say that a man with expertise in cavalry fighting who endures in a cavalry fight is less courageous than one who does so without this expertise?
	LACHES	That's my view.
	SOCRATES	And so also for one who has expertise with a sling or archery or any other skill and endures.
193c	LACHES	Of course.
	SOCRATES	And you will say that those who are willing to **dive down into a well** and endure work of this sort are more courageous if they are not good at it than those who are good at it?
	LACHES	Yes – what else could one say, Socrates?
	SOCRATES	Nothing at all, if that's what one thinks.

---

holds the better position the situation Socrates describes here resembles that of the allied army Laches helped lead at the battle of Mantinea in 418 BC. Laches and his fellow generals had placed their army on high ground outside Mantinea, where the Spartan army did not dare to attack them. But they were shaken by the criticism of their troops, who complained that they were letting the Spartans get away, and subsequently led the army down to the plain, where they were defeated; Laches died in the battle (Thucydides 5.65–74). The situation was complicated: the Spartans were diverting water to flood the territory of some of the allies in order to compel them to leave the high ground to stop the flooding, and Laches was only one of a number of generals on the scene. But given that Plato clearly alludes to Nicias' fatal mistake in Sicily (see the text box on pp. 105–6), it is likely that we are to see a similar allusion here. Laches and the other generals lacked the courage to keep the army on high ground in the face of the men's claim that doing so was cowardly. If Plato did indeed expect readers to think of the battle of Mantinea, this would help make sense of Laches' position here: he thought it was braver to fight down on the plain than on the high ground.

man in the opposing army Socrates and Laches thus agree that it is braver to fight against the odds than with them. This agreement will quickly get them (or at least Laches) into trouble – duplicating his experience at the battle of Mantinea (see the previous note).

dive down into a well presumably to unblock the well or retrieve something lost in it. Apparently men who were willing to do this provided a ready example of physical courage (Plato uses the same example at *Protagoras* 350a); we might think rather of people who work on skyscrapers.

	LACHES	This is indeed what I think.
	SOCRATES	Yet, Laches, such men do, I suppose, endure danger less prudently than those who do the same thing skilfully.
	LACHES	It does appear that way.
193d	SOCRATES	Now didn't imprudent daring and endurance appear to us to be shameful earlier on, as well as harmful?
	LACHES	Of course.
	SOCRATES	And it was agreed that courage is something admirable.
	LACHES	Yes, that was agreed.
	SOCRATES	But now, on the contrary, we are saying that this shameful thing, imprudent endurance, is courage.
	LACHES	We do seem to be doing so.
	SOCRATES	So do you think that this is an admirable way of speaking about this?
	LACHES	By Zeus, Socrates, it doesn't seem so to me.
193e	SOCRATES	So I suppose that, going by what you've said, you and I are **not in tune in the Dorian mode**, Laches: for our deeds aren't singing in the same key as our words. Someone could say, it seems, that our deeds are courageous, but no one would say the same of our words, if he heard what we were saying just now.
	LACHES	That's very true.
	SOCRATES	So what of it? Do you think this is an admirable state of affairs?
	LACHES	Not at all.
	SOCRATES	Now would you like us to agree to a certain extent with what we've been saying?
	LACHES	How much agreement do you mean, and with what?
194a	SOCRATES	Agreement with the argument that calls for endurance. So, if you will, let us too be steadfast and enduring in this investigation, so courage herself doesn't mock us for failing to seek her out courageously, if it does indeed turn out that courage is endurance.
	LACHES	I am not prepared to be the first to quit, Socrates, though I am quite unaccustomed to this sort of debate. I've actually been seized by
194b		a desire to win this verbal battle, and I'm really upset that I can't express what I'm thinking. For while I think I see what courage is, somehow or other it has escaped me, and I'm not able to pin it down with words.

---

not in tune in the Dorian mode   in a part of the dialogue not included above (188d–e), Laches had argued that a man ought to aim to keep his words and deeds in harmony, and in the noblest 'mode' (in modern musical terms, roughly, 'key') of Greek music, the Dorian mode. Socrates' and Laches' words are not courageous because they have failed to define courage; as Socrates notes a few lines later, their deeds are courageous inasmuch as they are steadfast in their effort to define courage.

1 How does Socrates prove that, according to Laches, courage is prudent endurance (by **192d**, p. 89)?

2 How does Socrates then show that this definition of courage can't be right (**192d–193e**, pp. 89–91)?

3 Where did Laches go wrong? Should he have rejected Socrates' argument that courage was prudent endurance? Or should he revise his views about the examples where he thought that those who acted less prudently acted more courageously?

4 One problem with the argument may be that it involves different sorts of knowledge that Socrates may (perhaps intentionally) run together:
   - prudence (the prudence that makes endurance admirable)
   - skill (for example, skill in fighting or diving)
   - calculation that the odds favour one in a given situation.

   Which of these types of knowledge, if any, makes an action less courageous?

5 Do you think that Socrates is trying to get at the truth about courage, or rather trying to undermine Laches' efforts to do so? If you had to defend what Socrates is doing here, what would you say?

Plato, forever old

In art Plato is invariably portrayed as an older man; even in David's famous picture of the death of Socrates (see p. 26), most identify the aged figure seated near a scroll as Plato, despite the fact that he would have been only 25 at the time. Plato was in fact the same age as some of the youths he depicts in conversation with Socrates. The discussions about how best to educate the young thus once applied to the young Plato himself. Plato the distinguished elder philosopher is shown here with a furrowed brow (note the horizontal wrinkles on his forehead, and the two vertical lines between his brows), similar to that which adorned many other intellectual portraits of the fourth century. This is what a deep thinker should look like, whether Plato looked like this or not.

First century AD Roman copy of a Greek original of the fourth century BC.

Socratic method

These days, what we call 'Socratic method' often involves a teacher asking leading questions to get students to provide the correct answers, answers the teacher already knows. This view of Socrates started with his enemies in antiquity. The **Thirty Tyrants** tried to outlaw Socratic questioning by passing a law against teaching 'the art of argument'. One of them warned Socrates as follows:

> Actually, Socrates, you are in the habit of asking about things that you already understand, for the most part. So don't ask about that sort of thing.
>
> (Xenophon, *Memorabilia* 1.2.36)

But it's pretty clear that this doesn't accurately describe what Socrates is about. Socrates may be asking leading questions, and he certainly has thought more about the questions he's asking than his **interlocutors** have, but if he is aiming to get them to produce the correct answer, to learn the truth about something, he does a horrible job of it. For Socrates' questions do not routinely lead to answers: they lead to contradictions.

In Gregory Vlastos' influential account of Socratic method, which Vlastos terms the **elenchus** (from a Greek word for 'examination'), Socrates' standard form of argument is as follows:

1   The interlocutor puts forward a thesis which Socrates considers false.

2   Socrates gets the interlocutor to agree to one or more further premises. They are ethical beliefs held already by the interlocutor. Socrates provides no argument in support of these premises: they are argued *from*, not argued *to*.

3   Socrates then argues, and the interlocutor agrees, that if one accepts these premises one must reject the initial thesis.

4   Socrates then claims that he has shown that the initial thesis is false (modified from Vlastos, *Socratic Studies*, p. 11 – see Further Reading).

One of the central mysteries about Socrates is why he can claim that (4) is true. After all, one could just as easily say that the initial thesis (1) was correct, and that one or more of the premises introduced (2) were incorrect, or that the logic of the argument (3) was at fault. Vlastos argues that Socrates has found, over the course of many arguments, that whenever an interlocutor puts forward an ethical claim that Socrates disagrees with (1), Socrates can always lead the interlocutor to admit to some other belief (2) that contradicts his initial, unSocratic claim (3). This repeated success provides Socrates with inductive support for his own beliefs, giving him good reason to conclude that it is the interlocutor who is wrong – that (1) must be wrong in the list above – and that it is Socrates who is correct.

So Socrates' moral beliefs are based on the fact that his own beliefs have repeatedly withstood this sort of argument: Socrates' set of beliefs, and only Socrates' set, is consistent. Socratic ethics are thus based not on self-evident truths (like those of mathematics), nor even on well-analysed popular beliefs (like the ethics of **Aristotle**), but on internal consistency confirmed in arguments with others. His beliefs are tested, but remain fallible: there is no logical impossibility that prevents Socrates from coming across an interlocutor who would find an inconsistency in Socrates' beliefs. This explains why Socrates can claim to know nothing important. And while he can find support for his beliefs in the views of everyone he argues with, his own views can still be paradoxical and radical, because most people haven't thought through the consequences of the various beliefs they hold. Through repeated conversations with others, Socrates has worked through his beliefs, and he has concluded that the only way to be consistent is to be radical.

In our case, we could fill in the argument as follows:

1   Laches suggests that courage is prudent endurance (**192d**, p. 89).

2   But Laches believes that those who prudently take risks (when the odds are with them) are less brave than those who take risks imprudently (when the odds are against them; **192e–193c**, pp. 89–91).

3   And Laches agrees that this contradicts his initial view (**193d–193e**).

Missing from the *Laches*, however, is any clear indication that Laches and Socrates reject the initial definition (step 4 in the scheme above). Obviously something has gone wrong, but Plato leaves us to figure out just what has gone wrong, presumably with help from the rest of the dialogue.

- Has Socrates proven that courage is not prudent endurance? Or has he only shown that Laches is confused about courage?
- Why is it so important that one's beliefs be consistent? Aren't good people sometimes torn between conflicting ethical claims?
- Does it make sense to expect that you can secure the agreement of all people to your ethical claims? If not, how should you confirm the validity of your beliefs about right and wrong?

Who's the author?

Socrates and Plato in Matthew Paris' fortune-telling book, c. 1250.

Socrates continued to appear in art of the Middle Ages and early Renaissance in the west, although artists had lost track of how he was portrayed in ancient art. Matthew Paris lacked ancient models, and also seems to have reversed the roles of Plato and Socrates: here it is Socrates rather than Plato who does the writing. Yet the drawing also, perhaps by chance, brilliantly captures what goes on in the Socratic dialogues of Plato. In Plato's writings Socrates is the character who dominates the stage, and we are left to wonder how much of what he says reflects Socrates' historical views, and how much has been whispered into his ear by Plato.

Courage as knowledge of what is fearful, and what not (194b–196c)

	SOCRATES	Well, my friend, a good hunter must keep up the pursuit and not give up.
	LACHES	Absolutely.
	SOCRATES	Now would you like us to summon Nicias here to the hunt, to see if he is more resourceful than we are?
194c	LACHES	I would – why wouldn't I?
	SOCRATES	Come on, then, Nicias, and help out, if you can, men who are your friends and have been swamped by a storm of argument. We're at a loss, as you can see. So tell us what you believe courage is, rescue us from our perplexity, and firm up your own view by putting it into words.
	NICIAS	Well, I've thought for some time that you two haven't done a very fine job of defining courage. I have heard you, Socrates, say something fine about this before, but you haven't made use of it here.
	SOCRATES	What's that, Nicias?
194d	NICIAS	I've often heard you say that each of us is good at things he is wise about, and if he is ignorant about something, he is not good at it.
	SOCRATES	That's quite true, by Zeus.
	NICIAS	So if the brave man is good, it's clear that he is wise.
	SOCRATES	Did you hear that, Laches?
	LACHES	I did hear it, but I don't really understand what he's saying.
	SOCRATES	Well, I do think I understand, and I think this man is saying that courage is some sort of wisdom.
	LACHES	What sort of wisdom, Socrates?
194e	SOCRATES	Why don't you ask him?
	LACHES	I will.
	SOCRATES	Come on then, Nicias, and tell him what sort of wisdom you take courage to be. For it's surely not about how to play the flute.
	NICIAS	Not at all.
	SOCRATES	Nor about how to play the lyre.
	NICIAS	Certainly not.
	SOCRATES	Well, which sort of knowledge is it? Knowledge of what?
	LACHES	This is absolutely the right way to question him, Socrates; let him say what sort of knowledge he claims it is.
	NICIAS	I say, Laches, that it is knowledge of what is fearful and what is hopeful, both in war and in everything else.
195a	LACHES	What a strange thing to say, Socrates!
	SOCRATES	What makes you say that, Laches?

LACHES	Because surely **knowledge and courage are different things**.
SOCRATES	That's not what Nicias says.
LACHES	No, by Zeus, it's not; and here he's spouting nonsense.
SOCRATES	Well, let's explain it to him rather than insulting him.
NICIAS	No, Socrates, I think Laches wants to make it look as if I have nothing to say, because that's how he appeared just now.
LACHES	Absolutely, Nicias: I'll try to make it clear that you have nothing to say. Take disease: don't doctors understand what's fearful about diseases? Or do you think it's courageous people who understand this? Or are doctors the ones you call courageous?
NICIAS	No, not at all.
LACHES	Nor is it farmers, I think. Yet they're the ones who understand what a farmer should fear, of course, just as all other workers understand what's fearful and what's hopeful in their own areas of expertise. But this doesn't make them one bit more courageous.
SOCRATES	What do you think of what Laches is saying, Nicias? He does seem to have a point.
NICIAS	Yes, he does have a point, but it's not true.
SOCRATES	How's that?
NICIAS	Because he thinks that doctors understand something about the sick beyond being able to say what's healthy and what's not. But surely **that's all they know**. And do you, Laches, hold that doctors understand whether someone should be more afraid of being healthy than of being sick? Don't you think that many are better off not recovering from sickness rather than recovering from it? Tell me this: do you say that everyone is better off living? Aren't many better off dead?
LACHES	I do agree with that.
NICIAS	Now do you think that the same things are fearful both to those who would gain by dying and to those who would gain by living?
LACHES	No, I don't.

195b, 195c, 195d are margin references corresponding to the text above.

---

knowledge and courage are different things Laches thus asserts the common sense idea that courage is not solely a matter of what you know. Nicias, on the other hand, is attempting to defend one of the **Socratic paradoxes**, the claim that virtue is knowledge: if you know the right thing to do, you always do it.

that's all they know Nicias may appear to have defined medicine rather narrowly, but he presumably includes knowledge of cures and prevention together with knowledge of diagnosis when he says that doctors know what is healthy. The crucial distinction is between knowing what is healthy for a person and what is best for him, all things considered. For example, a doctor would know how to prolong the life of a comatose patient with a terminal illness, but many would argue that it is better to allow such a patient to die sooner rather than later.

	NICIAS	Well, do you think that doctors or those in any other occupation understand this sort of thing? Or is it rather the person who understands what is fearful and what is not, the person I call courageous?
	SOCRATES	Laches, do you understand what he's saying?
195e	LACHES	I do: it's **seers** he calls courageous. For who else is going to know who is better off living than dying? So, Nicias, do you say that you are a seer, or agree that you are neither a seer nor courageous?
	NICIAS	What's this? Do you think that it's the seer who understands what's fearful and what's hopeful?
	LACHES	I do. Who else would it be?
	NICIAS	My good fellow, the man I'm talking about understands this far better. For a seer only needs to understand the signs that show what's going to happen – whether someone is going to die or get sick or lose money, or whether there's going to be a victory or defeat in war or some other contest. But whether it's going to be *better* for someone to experience one of these things rather than the other – how would a seer know this any better than anyone else?
196a		
	LACHES	Well, I don't understand what he's trying to say, Socrates. He's not making it clear who the courageous man is. He says it's not a seer or a doctor or anyone else. Perhaps he's saying it's some god who is courageous! At any rate, to me it looks as though Nicias isn't willing to be honest and admit that he's got nothing to say; he's twisting this way and that to hide his own confusion. You know, you and I could have done the same just now had we wanted to avoid appearing to contradict ourselves. If we were speaking in a courtroom, that would have made some sense. But why, in this sort of gathering, would someone fruitlessly try to make himself look good with such empty arguments?
196b		
196c	SOCRATES	I don't think that would make any sense, either, Laches. But let's look into this; Nicias may think that he has something to say, and may not be saying this just for the sake of argument. So let's ask him more clearly just what he has in mind. And if it becomes clear that he has a point, we'll agree with him; if not, we'll show him why we don't agree.

---

seers were specialists in reading the variety of signs sent by the gods, and were regularly consulted by individuals and communities. As we will see, armies routinely employed seers and consulted them before making major decisions (see the text box on pp. 105–6).

Courage and animals (196c–197e)

LACHES   Well, why don't you, Socrates, go ahead and ask the questions, if you'd like to? I've perhaps asked enough of them.

SOCRATES   There's no reason I shouldn't, as the questions will be asked on behalf of both of us.

LACHES   Absolutely.

SOCRATES   Tell me, Nicias, or rather tell *us*, since Laches and I are both sharing
196d   in the discussion: do you say that courage is knowledge of what is fearful and what is hopeful?

NICIAS   I do.

SOCRATES   And this isn't something that every man understands, since neither a doctor nor a seer knows this, and neither is courageous, unless he has this knowledge in addition to his professional expertise. Is that what you meant?

NICIAS   That's it.

SOCRATES   As the saying goes, then, **not every pig knows this** – nor would it be courageous.

NICIAS   Not in my view.

---

not every pig knows this   an ancient note on this passage says that the saying was 'as any dog or pig would know'.

196e	SOCRATES	It's clear then, Nicias, that you don't even believe that **the Crommyonian sow** was courageous. I don't say this as a joke; no, I think you must, if you say this, either deny that any animal is courageous, or else grant that an animal can be wise in some way. If you grant that, you'll have to say that lions and leopards and even boars understand something so difficult that few people understand it. In fact, anyone with your position on courage must say that **deer are by nature as courageous as lions**, and monkeys as courageous as bulls.
197a	LACHES	By the gods, Socrates, you've put that well! Tell us what you really think about this, too, Nicias. Do you say that these animals are wiser than we are – those animals which we all agree are courageous – or will you dare to contradict everyone and say that they aren't courageous?
	NICIAS	No, Laches, I call neither animals nor anyone else courageous when, out of ignorance, they don't fear what is fearful: I call them fearless and foolish. Or do you think that I call all children courageous,
197b		because they, in their ignorance, are afraid of nothing? No, I don't think that courage is the same thing as the lack of fear. I think that very few have courage and forethought, but that very many men and women and children and beasts possess boldness, daring and fearlessness without any forethought. They're the ones you and most people call courageous, but I call them bold; it's the prudent ones I've
197c		been talking about that I call courageous.
	LACHES	Behold, Socrates, what a fine job this man here thinks he's doing of making himself look good with this argument. It's people everyone agrees are courageous that he's trying to deprive of this honour.

---

the Crommyonian sow was a huge monster slain by the legendary hero Theseus. Monstrous wild boar were challenging opponents for many a hero of Greek myth. Real wild boar can weigh up to 200 pounds (90 kg); males sport tusks some 8 inches (20 cm) in length.

deer are by nature as courageous as lions apparently Socrates' argument goes like this: if courage is knowledge (as Nicias maintains), and deer and monkeys are as knowledgeable as lions and bulls (as Socrates assumes, presumably on the grounds that none of these animals is much wiser than the rest), then deer and monkeys must be as courageous as bulls and lions – even though it is only the latter who are normally considered courageous.

	NICIAS	But not you, Laches – take heart. For I say that you are wise, as is **Lamachus,** if you are indeed courageous, and so are many other Athenians.
	LACHES	I'll not dignify that with a reply, though I've got one ready; this way you won't be able to claim I'm a typical man from **Aexone.**
197d	SOCRATES	No, don't say anything, Laches. For you don't seem to realize that he's received this wisdom from **our friend Damon,** and Damon spends a great deal of time with **Prodicus,** who is thought to be the best of the sophists at distinguishing these sorts of terms.
	LACHES	And this sort of subtlety is fitting for a sophist – more so than for a man the city deems worthy of leading her.
197e	SOCRATES	Well, my blessed man, it is fitting that those who lead in the greatest things have a share in the greatest sort of prudence. And it seems to me that Nicias' view on this term, courage, is worth looking into.
	LACHES	Then look into it yourself, Socrates.

Lamachus was a prominent Athenian general who would go on to serve with Nicias during the Sicilian expedition (415–413), the disastrous campaign launched some time after the dramatic date of the *Laches*. During that expedition, when the Athenian generals realized that their Sicilian allies had lied about how much aid they could give, Lamachus advocated a sudden, bold strike against Syracuse, the most powerful city in Sicily, while Nicias recommended that the Athenians content themselves with a minor diplomatic victory and then sail home (Thucydides 6.47–9). Judging by this crucial example, at any rate, Lamachus was a far bolder general than Nicias; the cautious Nicias may well have regarded him as a good example of the thoughtless boldness that passes for courage among most people.

Aexone was Laches' home **deme** in Attica; according to an ancient note on this passage, people from Aexone were known for their abusive language. Laches recognizes the logic of Nicias' insult: if Laches and Lamachus are courageous, they must be wise; but Laches isn't wise, as shown by his failure to understand courage; therefore he must also be a coward!

our friend Damon earlier in the dialogue (in a passage not translated above) Nicias praised Socrates for introducing him to Damon as a teacher for his son. Nicias noted that Damon was not only a fine music teacher but a good all-round influence on the young (*Laches* 180c–d). But Damon, like other sophists, was also controversial; he was a teacher of the democratic Athenian statesman **Pericles**, and was ostracized (expelled from Athens for ten years) in 428, either as part of a political attack on Pericles, or because his own views were held suspect, or both. This legal action against a prominent intellectual is in some ways parallel to the trial of Socrates.

Prodicus of Ceos was a sophist best known, as this passage indicates, for distinguishing between terms close in meaning (like 'bold' and 'courageous'); Socrates lists him as a prominent and prosperous sophist at *Apology* **19e** (p. 35). He is also **Xenophon**'s source for the passage on the choice of Heracles we will encounter in the next chapter (pp. 108–23).

SOCRATES   That's what I'm about to do, my good fellow. But don't think that I'm letting you abandon your share in the argument; rather, pay attention and consider what's being said along with me.

LACHES   So be it, if you think that's necessary.

---

1   Laches here essentially gives up on the argument. Is he cowardly to do so? (See **194a** on p. 91.)

2   So are no animals brave? Aren't some braver than others? Or are some merely bolder than others?

3   Most think that Socrates himself would deny that animals can be courageous. Why then does he appear to attack Nicias' view that no animal is brave?

4   Has Nicias convinced you that courage is wisdom, that all it takes to be courageous is knowledge of some sort? Or do you side with Laches, who doesn't seem to be convinced? What could you say to try to counter Nicias' argument?

Socrates in Arabic

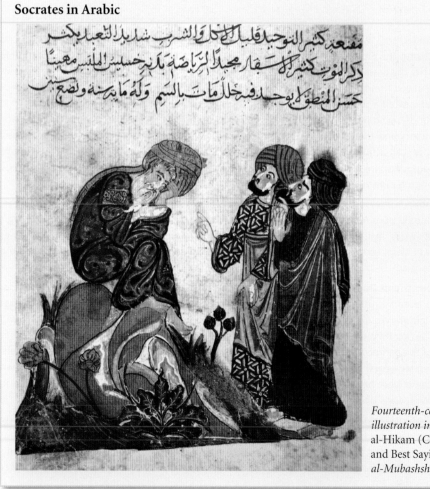

Fourteenth-century miniature illustration in Mukhtar al-Hikam (Choicest Maxims and Best Sayings) *by al-Mubashshir ibn Fātik.*

In the Arabic tradition, Socrates was one of the Seven Pillars of Wisdom, together with the other Greek sages, Thales, **Anaxagoras**, Anaximenes, Empedocles, Pythagoras and Plato. For the most part, he was more sage than philosopher, admired for the way he integrated his life and his thought rather than for his doctrines. A few Islamic thinkers criticized Socrates as a dangerous atheist, but for more he was a proto-Islamic saint unfairly condemned to death. Many sayings were attributed to Socrates – some of them assigned to other sages as well, and his philosophical views were something of a medley of various strands of Greek and Islamic thought. Yet much of what the Arabic authors admired can be found in our earliest sources, particularly the asceticism of their Socrates, and his commitment to a way of life beyond that espoused by conventional values. Our image, now in the Topkapi Palace in Istanbul, illustrates a text originally written in Damascus in the middle of the eleventh century. Here Socrates certainly looks sage-like. Deep in contemplation, he is approached by two students seeking to benefit from his superior wisdom.

- The Athenian Socrates delighted in public conversations in the centre of Athens, while the Islamic sage is shown in an isolated mountain locale, where disciples must approach him. Where do we expect to find wise people today, and what do we expect them to be doing?

Courage as a part of virtue (197e–199e)

	SOCRATES	I do think it's necessary to go on. Tell us again, Nicias, starting at the beginning. You know that **at the beginning** we were looking at courage as one part of virtue?
198a		
	NICIAS	Certainly.
	SOCRATES	So you too gave your answer on the assumption that it was one of the parts which, taken together, are called virtue?
	NICIAS	Of course.
	SOCRATES	Now are you and I talking about the same things? In addition to courage, I'm talking about moderation and justice and other things of that sort. Aren't you?
198b	NICIAS	Absolutely.
	SOCRATES	All right. We've agreed about this much, so let's consider what's fearful and what's hopeful, to make sure that all of us have the same things in mind. So we'll point out to you what we think about them; if you don't agree with us, explain why. We believe that fearful things

at the beginning at **190c**, p. 84.

are those which produce fear, while hopeful things do not produce fear. And it's not **evils** that have happened or evils that are present that produce fear, but expected evils. For we say that fear is an expectation of future evil. Isn't this your view, too, Laches?

198c LACHES   Very much so, Socrates.

SOCRATES   So you've heard our view, Nicias: we say that future evils are fearful, while future things that are not evil or are good are hopeful. Is this what you say about this, or is it something else?

NICIAS   That's what I say.

SOCRATES   And it is knowledge of these things that you term courage?

NICIAS   Exactly.

SOCRATES   Let's consider a third thing in addition to see if we all agree about it.

NICIAS   What's that?

198d SOCRATES   I'll explain. It seems to me and our friend here that whenever something can be known, there's not one form of knowledge about how things *have happened*, another about how things *are happening*, and another about how something that has not yet happened *will or may happen* in the best possible way. For example, take health: there nothing other than the single field of medicine oversees how things happen, have happened, and will happen. Farming does the same thing concerning things which grow in the earth. And no doubt the two of you could provide us first-hand evidence about war: it's the knowledgeable general who best foresees everything, especially what is going to happen. And he does not think that he should be subservient to the seer; he should rather rule him, since it is the general who best understands both what is happening and what will happen in war. Custom, too, arranges things this way: **the seer is not to lead the general, but the general to lead the seer.** Is this what we will say, Laches?

198e

199a

LACHES   We will.

---

evils translates the Greek adjective *kakos*, which can also mean 'harmful' or 'bad' in addition to 'evil'. In the present context, future evils are things or events which will prove to be harmful.

the seer is not to lead the general, but the general to lead the seer Greek armies sought out and paid highly regarded professional seers to read the signs from the gods before starting battle. There are indeed famous stories of generals avoiding battle when the seers said it was ill-advised, even when battle seemed the best option (Herodotus 9.61–2; Xenophon, *Anabasis* 5.5.1–2, 6.4.12–6.5.2) and of other generals ignoring omens to their own cost (Herodotus 9.41, 45). But usually a leader could find a way around bad omens, and more often than not the signs served to confirm a decision to fight or avoid battle rather than forcing a general to change his mind about what to do. See the text box opposite for Nicias' apparent willingness to give the seers too much power in Sicily.

Nicias in Sicily

The Athenian expedition in Sicily (415–413) met a tragic end, and in Thucydides' (*c*. 460–400) gripping account of that expedition Nicias emerges as a sort of tragic hero. Nicias had wisely opposed the expedition, but was nonetheless chosen to be one of the generals in command of it. The Athenians met with unexpectedly strong resistance, especially when they attempted to capture Syracuse, the most important city in Sicily. When an attack on the enemy lines outside Syracuse failed in the summer of 413, Nicias' fellow generals advised retreat. Nicias, however, opposed them, as he had reason to believe that the Syracusans were running low on money to pay their troops and that some in Syracuse wished to betray the city to Athens. In addition, Thucydides tells us that he feared that he would be put on trial at Athens if he led the army back without success, and would be blamed for defeat by the very soldiers who wanted the army to retreat now. 'Knowing the nature of the Athenians, he wished not to be destroyed by a dishonourable and unjust accusation made by them, but rather, if it had to be, to run the risk and die off the public stage' (Thucydides 7.48.4). Soon, however, the arrival of enemy reinforcements changed even Nicias' mind, and he too voted for retreat.

> When the Athenian generals saw that another army had joined their enemy and that their own situation was not improving but each day getting worse in every respect, and as they were particularly moved by the sickness among their soldiers, they were sorry that they had not departed earlier. Even Nicias no longer opposed them as he had before, save to the extent of **rejecting a public vote**. And so they gave orders that all would sail off as secretly as possible, and that they were to be prepared to depart when the signal was given. When everything was ready and they were about to sail off, there was an eclipse of the moon, which was then full. This weighed heavily on the minds of the majority of the Athenians, and they bid the generals to put off the retreat. Nicias – who was rather too susceptible to religious matters of this sort – said that he would not even allow them to discuss moving before the 27-day delay the seers had called for.
>
> (Thucydides 7.50.2–4)

---

rejecting a public vote   an open vote would have alerted the Syracusans to the Athenian plan to retreat.

This delay was fatal, as the Syracusans first defeated the Athenian fleet and then destroyed the Athenian army when the Athenians attempted to retreat overland. Nicias himself finally surrendered, but was murdered by his captors. Thucydides' last words about Nicias describe him as the man 'who, of all the Greeks in my time, least deserved to meet with such misfortune, as in all he did he recognized virtue as his guide' (7.86.5).

- As general, then, Nicias let himself be led by the seers. Was his failure one of courage?
- Now that you've read of the fates of Nicias and Laches (see the note at **193a**, p. 90), do you have any ideas about why Plato chose to have Socrates discuss courage with these two? Does their inability to define courage here shed light on their failures in the field?

	SOCRATES	All right. Do you, Nicias, agree with us that one and the same type of knowledge covers a given set of things, whether they will happen, are happening, or have happened?
	NICIAS	I do – that's how it seems to me, Socrates.
199b	SOCRATES	Excellent. And courage is knowledge of what is fearful and what is hopeful, in your view, right?
	NICIAS	Yes.
	SOCRATES	And it's been agreed that fearful things are future evils, while hopeful things are future goods?
	NICIAS	Of course.
	SOCRATES	And the same knowledge covers the same things, whether they are going to happen or **whatever state they may be in**?
	NICIAS	That is so.
199c	SOCRATES	So courage isn't only knowledge of fearful and hopeful things. For it doesn't only cover good and evil things that *will* happen, but also goods and evils that *are* happening or *have* happened or whatever state they may be in, just like other sorts of knowledge.
	NICIAS	It seems so.
199d	SOCRATES	So your answer, Nicias, gave us more or less a third of courage, though we were asking you what the whole of courage was. And it now seems that, according to what you're saying, courage is not only knowledge of fearful or hopeful things; rather, courage would cover pretty much all goods and evils of any sort, or so you're saying now. Is this your new position, Nicias, or do you mean something else?
	NICIAS	That's what I think, Socrates.

---

whatever state they may be in   Plato thus allows for evils that 'may happen' or the like, in addition to definite past, present, and future evils.

SOCRATES	Splendid. So do you think that a person like this would lack any part of virtue, if he knew all good things and every way that they come to pass, will come to pass, and have come to pass – and knew the same about evils? Do you think that this man would lack moderation or justice or piety, given that he alone can take adequate precautions about what is fearful and what not and can secure good things, knowing as he does how to behave correctly regarding both gods and men?

199e

NICIAS	You seem to have a point, Socrates.
SOCRATES	So, Nicias, what you've been talking about just now isn't *a part of virtue*, but the *whole of virtue*?
NICIAS	It appears so.
SOCRATES	And yet we said that courage was one part of virtue.
NICIAS	We did say that.
SOCRATES	But the thing under discussion doesn't appear to be one part.
NICIAS	It seems not.
SOCRATES	So, Nicias, we haven't discovered what courage is.
NICIAS	It appears that we haven't.

In the final few pages of the dialogue Laches shows how pleased he is that Nicias has been shown to know nothing about courage, despite all his study with Damon (see **197d**, p. 101). Nicias for his part attacks Laches for being more interested in exposing his failure than in acknowledging his own ignorance about something any decent man should understand. Nicias says he will return to Damon for more guidance on these matters. Laches suggests, and Nicias agrees, that the boys should study with Socrates rather than with them, but Socrates demurs: he needs as much help as any. Rather, he suggests that all present should devote themselves to finding the best teachers. All agree to meet again on the next day to discuss this further (*Laches* 200a–201c).

Nicias and Socrates seem to have discovered the whole of virtue – knowledge of good and evil. But rather than being pleased with this discovery, they conclude that they have failed to discover courage, because courage is only one part of virtue. This raises some questions:

1 Why do Socrates and Nicias declare failure (their failure to define courage) rather than declaring success (their apparent success in defining virtue)?

2 Does virtue have parts? That is, do you believe that a person can truly be good in one respect but not in others?

3 How would you describe the role Socrates has played in this discussion? Has he helped to articulate the strengths and weaknesses of his interlocutor's views? Or has he just said whatever it takes to prove his interlocutors wrong?

4 Is the *Laches* meant to solve problems or pose them?

---

4 Xenophon's Socrates

Introduction

We now turn to **Xenophon's** portrayal of Socrates. The *Memorabilia*, Xenophon's longest Socratic work, is devoted largely to showing how valuable a companion Socrates was to all who associated with him. Xenophon provides us with a large number of fairly short conversations between Socrates and a wide range of **interlocutors**, and on a wide range of themes. But among the most important lessons his Socrates offers is the value of self-control (*enkrateia*). Excerpted here is one of Socrates' most ambitious lessons on self-control, directed at a follower of his who was notably deficient in that area; it culminates in a famous passage about the hero Heracles.

Self-control and leadership (Xenophon, *Memorabilia* 2.1.1–9)

[1] In my view, by saying the following things he encouraged his companions to train themselves to control their desire for food and drink and sex and sleep, and to endure cold and heat and hard work. He recognized that one of his companions had little self-control about such things, and so he said to him, 'Tell me, **Aristippus**,

---

Aristippus   of Cyrene, a Greek city in North Africa, was credited with founding a school of thought promoting **hedonism**, the idea that pleasure is the goal of human life. He was born by 440 and survived well into the fourth century. **Aristippus** is said to have spent considerable time at the court of the Sicilian tyrants Dionysius I and/or Dionysius II, who ruled Syracuse, the leading city in Sicily, during the first half of the fourth century. Here, according to the anecdotes that have come down to us, Aristippus cleverly used his access to the tyrant to support a luxurious lifestyle. **Plato** made three visits to Syracuse himself, but tried a different tack, as he aimed to convert the tyrants to philosophy. He succeeded only in getting himself imprisoned by the tyrants on at least two occasions (see Plato's *Seventh Letter* for the details). At *Memorabilia* 3.8, Aristippus will attempt, unsuccessfully, to get revenge on Socrates for his treatment in our passage.

---

if you had to take over **the education of two young men**, to make one capable of ruling, and the other not even interested in ruling, how would you educate each? Would you like us to start our investigation of this with their nourishment, given that it is one of the elements involved?'

Aristippus said, 'Nourishment does seem to me to be fundamental; one cannot live without nourishment.'

[2] 'Won't both probably want to get hold of food at mealtimes?'

'Yes,' he said, 'they probably will.'

'So which of them would we want to train to take care of urgent business rather than indulge his belly?'

'By Zeus,' he said, 'that would be the one educated to rule, so public business is not neglected during his rule.'

'And when they want to drink, are we to give the ability to hold off from drinking to the same one?'

'Absolutely,' he said.

[3] 'And to which would we give self-control regarding sleep, so that he is able to go to bed late, get up early, and go without sleep, if necessary?'

'To the same one again.'

'And what about self-control regarding lust,' he said, 'so as to not be hindered by that if something else needs to be done?'

'That too would be for the same one,' he said.

'And what about not evading hard work, but being willing to stick to it? Which one would we give this to?'

'This too,' Aristippus said, 'would be for the one being educated to rule.'

'What about learning any lesson required in order to overcome one's opponents – which would we give this to?'

---

the education of two young men Socrates here discusses the sorts of lessons that would normally be handed over, then as now, within families, but goes on to draw out more philosophical points about the value of self-control. His suggestion that rulers could be educated differently from the ruled is rather anti-democratic: in a democracy all citizens were supposed to take turns ruling and being ruled. But as a matter of fact, at Athens most education was private, meaning that the wealthy (who would more often aspire to rule) could afford far more of it than the poor, as only they could pay professional teachers (especially the expensive **sophists**), and only they had free time to devote to education. As this passage goes on, though, it becomes clear that Socrates would have all people educated in self-control, not only rulers.

'Far more still, by Zeus, to the one being educated to rule,' he said. 'For **none of the other qualities has any value without this sort of lesson**.'

[4] 'And don't you think that someone educated in this way is less prone to be taken unaware by his opponents than is any other being? For aren't some creatures, even if they are very timid, lured on by their bellies when their desire to eat drives them towards the bait, while others are trapped by drink?'

'Absolutely,' he said.

'And aren't others, as quail and partridges, trapped by lust? Led on towards **the call of the female** by their desire and hope for sex, they fail to consider the dangers and fall into traps.'

He agreed to this too.

[5] 'Don't you think that it's shameful for a man to be subject to the same things that happen to the most foolish beasts? For example, adulterers go into **enclosed places**, knowing the risk for the adulterer and the things the law threatens him with: being trapped, captured, and **subjected to abuse**. Although the adulterer is faced with so many evils and so much disgrace, and though there are many ways to **sate one's desire for sex without any risk**, nevertheless he is led into danger. Isn't this the mark of an utterly worthless man?'

'So it seems to me,' he said.

[6] 'Given that most of the most important activities for men take place outdoors – warfare and farming and many of the rest – doesn't it seem to you that most men are utterly careless when they fail to train themselves to deal with cold and heat?'

He agreed to this as well.

---

none of the other qualities has any value without this sort of lesson Aristippus is a true follower of Socrates at least in this sense: he regards learning as the most important quality for a man to pursue.

the call of the female ancient hunters, like modern ones, imitated the call of their prey to lure them to their deaths.

enclosed places Greek women were expected to remain at home most of the time, precisely to protect them from adultery, and hence the would-be adulterer would have to sneak into the house to fulfil his desires.

subjected to abuse a husband who caught a man with his wife could not only kill the adulterer but subject him to humiliating physical abuse, such as shoving a vegetable up his anus and singeing and plucking his pubic hair (**Aristophanes**, *Clouds* 1083). This abuse was meant to compensate for the adulterer's attempt to humiliate the husband.

sate one's desire for sex without any risk prostitution, which was legal in the ancient world, would have been one way to do so; slave owners also had sexual access to their slaves.

'And one who is going to rule must practise enduring such things easily.'

'Absolutely,' he said.

[7] 'And if we group those who are self-controlled regarding all these things with those who are able to rule, shall we group those unable to do these things with those with no claim to rule?'

He agreed to this as well.

'What then? Now that you know how to classify each type, have you ever considered which type you are?'

[8] 'I have,' said Aristippus. 'By no means do I group myself with those who want to rule. Given how hard a task it is even to provide yourself with all you need, it seems to me that only a complete fool would not content himself with taking care of himself, but take on the additional task of providing his fellow citizens with whatever they need. How could it not be utter foolishness to lack many of the things you want yourself when you are in charge of the city, and to **risk being put on trial** if you do not accomplish everything the city wants you to? [9] For cities treat their leaders like I treat my slaves. I think that my servants should provide me with an enviable livelihood, but touch none of it themselves, while cities believe that their rulers should provide them with as many goods as possible while keeping away from those goods themselves. I, then, would put those who want to have a lot of trouble themselves and provide others with a lot of trouble, with the rulers. I group myself with those who want to lead lives that are as easy and pleasant as possible.'

1. Just why is self-control so essential, according to Xenophon's Socrates?

2. Why do you think Socrates proposes the experiment of training one man to rule and one to be ruled? Does he think that only rulers need self-control? Or do his arguments really apply to both rulers and subjects?

3. Why does Aristippus say that he doesn't want to rule?

4. Greek education put a high emphasis on athletic training. Does such training help to promote the skills of self-control that Socrates promotes here?

5. Modern politicians often find themselves embroiled in sex scandals and the like. Do we expect our leaders to be more self-controlled than other people? Should we?

---

risk being put on trial Aristippus seems to have Athens in mind. At Athens, all office holders were subject to judicial scrutiny upon leaving office, and politically motivated lawsuits were common, making politics a risky business. Compare *Apology* **31d–32a** (pp. 61–2) and *Laches* **191d** (p. 87).

The Oracle of Apollo at Delphi

The temple of Apollo at Delphi.

The shrine and oracle of Apollo lies in beautiful mountainous terrain some 180 kilometres (112 miles) north-west of Athens. Here Chaerephon, according to Plato, was told that there was no one wiser than Socrates (*Apology* **21a**, p. 39). Xenophon, however, tells a rather different version of the story.

> Chaerephon once enquired about me at **Delphi** in the presence of many people, and Apollo replied that there was no man freer or more just or more moderate than I.
>
> (Xenophon, *Apology of Socrates* 14)

Xenophon's oracle thus makes no reference to wisdom, the single trait mentioned in Plato's version. Nor does Xenophon's Socrates make the oracle the spur to a philosophical mission spent questioning others about **virtue** – the very mission that, in Plato's account, led so many to hate Socrates.

It is this sort of divergence in our sources that has led scholars to despair of ever rediscovering the historical truth about Socrates. Certainly Plato's Socrates is more humble and profound, and the list of virtues Xenophon's Socrates gives us is both more pedestrian and more arrogant. In fact one of Xenophon's main points in his *Apology* was to show that Socrates had no intention of securing his acquittal; he had decided that it was time for him to die, and arrogantly proclaimed his own virtue, and his own understanding of the best life. Thus in Xenophon the oracle story confirms Socrates' arrogance, rather than explaining why people hated Socrates.

Whatever else they were doing, Plato and Xenophon told the oracle story in a way that fitted their own literary goals. This doesn't mean there couldn't have been a real oracle, only that our attempts to reconstruct it must take into account how both Xenophon and Plato shaped the story of the oracle to meet their own ends.

- Does it matter if we can reconstruct what actually happened at Delphi, and what Socrates made of it? Why or why not?

Aristippus, a stranger everywhere (2.1.10–20)

[10] Then Socrates said, 'So would you like us to investigate whether it is the rulers or the ruled who live more pleasant lives?'

'Absolutely,' he said.

'Let's begin with the peoples known to us. In Asia the **Persians rule, and the Syrians and Phrygians and Lydians are ruled**. In Europe the **Scythians rule, while the Maeotians are ruled**. In **Libya**, the Carthaginians rule, while the Libyans are ruled. So which of these have more pleasant lives, do you think? Or consider the Greeks, as you're one of them: which seem to you to have more pleasant lives, those with power or those they have power over?'

[11] 'But,' said Aristippus, 'I don't consign myself to slavery, either. No, I think that between these things there is a middle path, which I attempt to travel: it leads neither through rule nor through slavery but through freedom, and it is the best path to happiness.'

Persians rule, and the Syrians and Phrygians and Lydians are ruled the Persians, a people whose heartland lies in modern Iran, ruled a vast empire stretching from Afghanistan to Egypt that included ancient Syria (modern Syria, Lebanon and Israel), and Phrygia and Lydia (two regions in Asia Minor). As most Greeks saw it, the Persians had once been a tough, simple, virtuous mountain people, but came to lead luxurious, soft lives once they conquered their empire. It would thus be hard for Aristippus to deny that they had more pleasant lives than their subjects.

Scythians rule, while the Maeotians are ruled the Scythians were a nomadic people who lived mainly in what is now Ukraine; the Maeotians were a related people living to the east of the Scythians around the sea of Azov (the Maeotian Lake in ancient terms), in the south of Russia.

Libya ancient Libya included all of North Africa west of Egypt. Carthage, a city near modern Tunis, was founded by people from ancient Phoenicia (Lebanon); the Libyans were the inhabitants native to the areas colonized by these Phoenicians. Aristippus was from Cyrene, a Greek city in North Africa, so would have known this area well.

[12] 'Well,' said Socrates, 'if this path which leads neither through rule nor through slavery also does not pass by men, perhaps you'd have a point. But if you plan to live among men, and yet neither to rule nor to be ruled nor to serve those who rule, I think you can see that those who are stronger know how to treat the weaker like slaves and make them howl.

[13] 'Or have you never noticed those who **cut down the crops and trees** that others have sown and planted and who use every means to besiege those who are weaker when those people are unwilling to serve them, until they persuade the weaker people to choose slavery instead of fighting against those who are stronger than they are? And don't you know that individuals who are courageous and capable enslave and profit from those who are unmanly and incapable?'

'But, in order to avoid suffering that, I do not confine myself to any one community, but am everywhere a **stranger**.'

[14] And Socrates said, 'Now that's a clever move! For ever since **the deaths of Sinis, Sciron and Procrustes**, no one mistreats strangers any more. No, while those who live as citizens in cities nowadays pass laws to avoid being wronged, and seek out friends to help them out, in addition to those bound to them by family ties; while they surround cities with walls and acquire weapons to ward off those who would do them wrong, and, what's more, also secure allies from outside; and though these people, despite all these precautions, are still done wrong, [15] you, though you have none of these advantages and spend a great deal of time on the road, where most wrongdoing takes place; though you have less status than any citizen in every city you come to; though you are **the sort of man** whom those looking to do injustice most often attack; nevertheless, because you are a stranger,

---

cut down the crops and trees   invading Greek armies regularly ravaged the farmlands of their opponents in this way. The Spartans routinely did this to the territory of Athens during the **Peloponnesian War**.

stranger   the Greek word is *xenos*; in addition to referring to someone from out of town, it can refer to an out-of-town guest or host, and thus has somewhat warmer connotations than our 'stranger'. But as Greece was not a nation-state, Greeks from one city did not enjoy anything like full rights in other Greek cities. Most Greeks saw their identities as closely tied up with their home city, and exile was a very stiff punishment. Aristippus' position is therefore most unusual.

the deaths of Sinis, Sciron and Procrustes   the legendary Athenian hero Theseus killed these three, who were said to attack travellers on the roads leading to Athens. Procrustes, the most famous of them, was said to be a rogue blacksmith who would offer travellers a place to stay but then make them fit the bed he offered them by cutting off their feet if they were too long or stretching them out if they were too short (he had two beds of different lengths in case he found someone who fit one). Hence today we use the term *procrustean* of a rule or procedure that arbitrarily disregards individual differences.

the sort of man   an apparent reference to Aristippus' riches and easy-going lifestyle, which would have made him an easy target.

you think that you will not be wronged? Are you confident because cities offer safe passage for strangers when they come and go? Or because you think that you would be the sort of slave who would be of no use to any master? For who would want to have someone in his home who wasn't willing to work, but enjoyed the most luxurious lifestyle? [16] So let's consider this too, how masters deal with slaves of this sort. Don't they control the lust of their slaves by starving it? And don't they prevent them from stealing anything by barring them from any place where there is something worth taking? Don't they fetter them to prevent them from running off? And don't they beat the laziness out of them? Or how do you deal with slaves when you learn that you've got one like this?'

[17] 'I punish them,' he said, 'with every kind of hardship, until I force them to slave away. But, Socrates, those who are educated in the royal art, something you, I think, consider to be happiness indeed – how does their willingness to go hungry and thirsty and suffer from cold and lack of sleep and every other form of hardship distinguish them from those who are forced to suffer such things? I don't see how it makes any difference if the same skin is beaten willingly or unwillingly, or if one's whole body is assailed by every sort of torture willingly or unwillingly – except for the fact that the person who willingly puts up with these pains suffers from stupidity as well.'

[18] 'What do you mean, Aristippus?' Socrates said. 'Don't you think that there's a big difference between doing this willingly or unwillingly, since someone who is willing to go hungry can eat whenever he wants to, someone willing to go thirsty can drink when he wants to, and so on for the rest, while one who does so unwillingly cannot stop doing so when he wants to? So the one who works away willingly is happy, since he works with hope of a good result, just as those hunting wild beasts enjoy their efforts because of their hope of capturing one. [19] In such cases the prize for hard work isn't very valuable, but what of those who work in order to gain good friends, or to defeat their enemies, or to develop bodies and souls capable of running their own households well, helping their friends, and benefiting their cities? Doesn't one have to acknowledge that these men enjoy working for such goals and enjoy happy lives, pleased with themselves, and praised and envied by others?

[20] 'What's more, taking it easy and enjoying the pleasures of the moment doesn't get one's body into good shape, as trainers tell us, nor does it provide the **soul** with any worthwhile knowledge; it is activities which require endurance that allow one to achieve noble and good things, as good men tell us. **Hesiod** says somewhere:

Hesiod was a poet active around 700 BC, around the same time as Homer. Socrates quotes lines 287–92 from Hesiod's *Works and Days*, a poem in which he advises his wayward brother to work hard and act justly.

Easy it is to choose to be base; men do so in droves.

That pathway is smooth, and is found close at hand.

But the immortal gods make us sweat to win virtue:

Long and steep is the path up to reach her,

And rough it is, at first. But reach the peak

And what was hard becomes easy.

'And **Epicharmus** testifies to this as well in the following:

For all good things the gods demand we toil.

'And in another place he says:

Wretch, seek not a soft life, lest you have a hard one.'

1 What sort of life does Aristippus hope to live? Is it possible to live independently of others – neither ruling nor being ruled? Would doing so be admirable?

2 What kind of life would one with Aristippus' values choose to lead today?

3 Why, according to Socrates, is it better to go hungry voluntarily rather than to do so involuntarily?

4 Socrates here presents a rather bleak view of a world in which the strong prey on the weak. But his argument is at least as much a refutation of Aristippus as it is a demonstration of Socrates' own views (see text box on Socratic method on pp. 93–4). Is the nasty world Socrates envisions here somehow a consequence of Aristippus' views, or does it simply offer a realistic view of the way things are?

5 Xenophon's Socrates appeals to poets to back up his arguments (and, in the next section, he quotes a sophist). Whom would a modern thinker appeal to? And what do our differing sources of authority tell us about how our society differs from that of Socrates' Athens?

Epicharmus was a Greek comic playwright from Sicily who was active early in the fifth century BC. His works survive only in fragments, largely in lines quoted by other authors, as Xenophon does here in quoting fragments 36 and 37.

The low road or the high road

The Choice of Hercules, *1596, by Annibale Carracci.*

The story of Heracles (or Hercules, in the Latinized version of his name) at the Crossroads has been a popular theme in western art. Here a youthful but already muscular Heracles is torn between the noble Virtue and the scantily clad Vice, whose 'clothing revealed all her charms' (*Memorabilia* **2.1.22**, p. 119). Virtue points to her steep path upward, a path resembling the tough climb to virtue Hesiod described in the passage quoted on the previous page. Vice for her part points to the low road, here associated with the pleasures of music and the theatre. In the left foreground a muscular author (Xenophon? **Prodicus**?) takes notes on the scene.

- Does Heracles' pose indicate which goddess he will follow?

Heracles at the Crossroads (2.1.21–34)

Plato famously has Socrates tell myths on a number of occasions, most notably the accounts of the underworld and afterlife in the *Gorgias* (523a–527) and the *Phaedo* (107c–115a), the somewhat similar myth of Er at the close of the *Republic* (10.614b–621d), and the myth of the winged soul in the *Phaedrus* (246a–249d). In the continuation of our passage from the *Memorabilia*, we see Xenophon engage in a somewhat similar manoeuvre by having Socrates summarize a sophistic account of an event in the life of the Greek hero, Heracles. The Platonic myths, with their seemingly confident depictions of the soul's journey after death, are generally thought to go well beyond anything the historical Socrates would have said. But in both authors the resort to story-telling rather than argument is presumably motivated by a desire to reach as large an audience as possible.

[21] 'And **Prodicus** the wise, in his essay on **Heracles**, which he's **presented on many occasions**, puts forward the same view about virtue. It goes something like this, as far as I remember.

Prodicus   was a prominent sophist and a contemporary of Socrates; we have met him already in the *Apology* (**19e**, p. 35) and *Laches* (**197d**, p. 101). As no works of his survive, this account of Heracles at the Crossroads, if it accurately reflects Prodicus' original essay, would be essential for reconstructing his thought. The piece was well known enough for Plato to allude to it at *Symposium* 177b. But Prodicus is elsewhere associated mainly with efforts to distinguish between near synonyms, something our passage does not concern itself with. And it is not clear how closely Xenophon's Socrates sticks to the original composition by Prodicus (note his hesitations at sections **21** and **34**). Certainly the basic thrust of the argument here is in keeping with what Xenophon's Socrates argues on his own behalf elsewhere.

Heracles   was the most popular of Greek heroes. His most famous exploits were his labours; one Greek term for this sort of ennobling labour is *ponos*, a term which occurs frequently in the passage above, where it is usually translated as 'hard work'. These labours made Heracles an obvious example for a lecture on the value of such hard work. Heracles did, however, also like his pleasures. In Aristophanes' *Clouds* (1051) it is pointed out that Heraclean baths are pleasant warm ones, something which seemed corrupt in terms of conservative values; and in Euripides' *Alcestis* Heracles is something of a drunk, though a heroic one. Hence one can well imagine a youthful Heracles being tempted by Vice.

Another follower of Socrates, **Antisthenes**, wrote works in which Heracles was represented as a moral exemplar, thanks to his laborious pursuit of virtue. Antisthenes was as opposed to hedonism as Aristippus was devoted to it: Socrates' thought could be developed in very different directions, rather as Heracles could be depicted either as a man of toil or as a man driven by his appetites.

presented on many occasions   a piece like this one would be read aloud in public performance; one venue for this was competition at the same sort of festivals that hosted athletic contests.

'Heracles had left boyhood behind and was coming of age, at the point when young men become independent and reveal whether they will turn their lives towards the path of virtue or that of vice. He had gone out to a quiet spot and sat down, at a loss as to which path he should take. [22] And two women of larger than mortal stature appeared and approached him; one of them had a seemly beauty, and a noble nature; her body was adorned with purity, her eyes with modesty; her bearing was dignified and she was dressed in white. The other was well-fed, fleshy and voluptuous; her face was made up to make her complexion appear more radiant and rosy than it really was, and she carried herself so as to appear more upright than she naturally was; her eyes were all a-flutter, and her clothing revealed all her charms. She kept looking herself over, and watched to see if anyone was admiring her; she would often look at her own shadow.

[23] 'As they neared Heracles, the first one continued at the same pace, but the other wanted to get there first, and so she ran up to Heracles and addressed him as follows.

'"I see, Heracles, that you do not know which path your life should take. If you make me your friend, I will lead you along the most pleasant and most easy path; there is no delight you will not taste, nor will your life encounter any hardship. [24] First off, you will not worry about wars or other troubles; your only concern will be what pleasing food or drink you can find, what delightful sight or sound, or smell or touch; **what boy** will cheer you most with his company; how you can sleep most softly; and how to get all of this without any hard work. [25] And if there's any hint that these joys will be in short supply, fear not that I will drive you to acquire them by toilsome labours of body and soul; no, you will benefit from the work done by others, nor will you leave anything undone if it can bring you profit. For I give my companions the authority to help themselves to everything."

[26] 'And when he'd heard this, Heracles said, "Woman, what is your name?"

'She replied, "My friends call me Happiness, though those who hate me give me the nickname Vice."

[27] 'Meanwhile the other woman drew near and said, "I too have come to you, Heracles, because I know **your parents**, and I observed your character during

---

what boy Vice thus promises Heracles a boyfriend. Among many Athenian aristocrats, the most idealized romantic relationships were those between young adult men and teenage boys. In one myth Heracles leaves behind the heroes on the *Argo* to search for his beloved Hylas, a young man who has disappeared (kidnapped by nymphs, who also found Hylas irresistible). But contrast Virtue's attitude at section **30** (p. 122).

your parents Heracles' mother was Alcmene, wife of Amphitryon; his father was Zeus himself, who visited Alcmene while disguised as Amphitryon. Virtue implies, in keeping with traditional Greek thinking, that noble parents like this will produce noble offspring.

your upbringing. This leads me to expect that, if you turn to my path, you will become a most mighty doer of fine and noble deeds, and make me appear still more honoured and glorious for my good deeds. I will not deceive you by starting out with promises of pleasure, but will tell you the truth about how the gods have arranged things.

[28] "'The gods give nothing fine or good to men unless men devote themselves to hard work. If you want the gods to favour you, **you must serve the gods**; if you want to have friends who love you, you must benefit your friends. If you desire to be honoured by a city, you must help that city; if you want all of Greece to admire your virtue, you must attempt to do well by Greece. If you want the earth to bear you abundant crops, you must work the earth, and if you believe you need to grow rich by herding animals, you must care for those animals. If you aim to gain power through war and want to be able to keep your friends free and get the better of your enemies, you must study the arts of war under those who understand them, and practise using these arts aright. And if you want your body to be powerful, you must accustom it to serve your mind and train it with hard work and sweat.'"

[29] 'Here Vice took over, Prodicus says. "Do you realize, Heracles, how hard and long a path towards enjoyment this woman is showing you? I will lead you along an easier and shorter path to happiness."

Virtue battling Vice

Where most artists, like Carracci (see p. 117), give us a rather static scene with Virtue and Vice posing for Heracles, the German Renaissance artist Albrecht Dürer produced an action-packed version in the engraving opposite. Vice is depicted lying in the lap of a **satyr**, one of the half-goat, half-man creatures known for their sexual appetites. The toddler fleeing to the right is Cupid (Love/Lust), who has presumably been busy with the couple on the left. Virtue clearly intends to give Vice a rather more physical version of the rhetorical beating she delivers in Prodicus' story.

- What is Heracles (the figure holding the staff) going to do?

---

you must serve the gods   the Greek gods were anthropomorphic and were thought to behave as humans do. A fundamental theme in interactions between humans and gods as among humans was reciprocity. Rather than obeying some abstract code of behaviour, or aiming at the 'golden rule' of doing unto others as we *would like them* to do unto us, conventional Greek ethics and religion called upon people to treat others as they *had in fact* been treated by them. A good man helps his friends and harms his enemies; so too the gods aid their followers and harm those who slight them.

Hercules at the Crossroads, *1598, engraving by Albrecht Dürer.*

[30] 'But Virtue said, "You wretch, what good are you? And what do you know about pleasure, you who are willing to do nothing for it? You cannot tolerate the desire for pleasure, but sate yourself before you can desire anything, eating before you are hungry, drinking before you are thirsty. To enjoy eating, you arrange for gourmet chefs; to enjoy drinking, you acquire the most expensive wines and run around looking for ice water to cool them with in summer. To enjoy sleeping, you not only get yourself soft bedding but even a bed that rocks – for you don't long for sleep because you're tired out, but because you've got nothing better to do.

You force yourself to have sex before you need it, leaving nothing untried and **treating men as women**. Thus you educate your friends by acting outrageously at night and sleeping away the better part of the day.

[31] "'Though immortal yourself you have been cast out from the gods, and are without honour among good men. The most pleasant of all sounds, praise, you never hear, nor do you ever see the most pleasant sight, for you never see

Heracles and Athena

Interior of a red-figure cup by Douris, c. 480 BC.

Heracles at the Crossroads is not a theme in ancient art. But we do find Heracles guided, if not by Virtue, then by Athena, the goddess of warfare and wisdom who stood by so many Greek heroes. Here Heracles, wearing his trademark lion's skin, gets a well-deserved drink from Athena. She has put down her helmet, though she still holds her owl and spear; she is garbed in the divine *aegis*, which protects her from attack. Her dignified beauty resembles that which Prodicus attributes to Virtue. Heracles drinks from a heroic-sized cup, but is he telling Athena he wants more, or that she's given him enough?

- Who inspires heroes today?

treating men as women Virtue thus appears to reject sex between men, though her point may be that a man should not take an *adult* man as a passive sexual partner. In the Greek way of seeing things, one's role in a sexual relationship was at least as important as the gender of one's sexual partner. If one was active – if, in concrete terms, one did the penetrating – one was manly; if one was passive, one was effete. Many Greek men regarded male teenagers not only as the most attractive male sexual partners, but as the most appropriate ones, since they were not yet fully mature men and so were not as compromised by playing a passive role. But in Xenophon's *Symposium*, Socrates argues that relationships between older men and the younger men they find themselves attracted to should not be sexually consummated, because sex would ruin any chance for a lasting friendship between the two (*Symposium* 8).

any noble deed you yourself have done. Who would trust what you say? Who would help you when you need something? Who in their right mind would be rash enough to join your revellers? While young their bodies are weak, and when they've become old their minds lack sense; nourished in easy luxury through their youth, they pass old age in hardship and squalor, ashamed of what they have done and burdened by what they are doing; they run through all their pleasures in youth, and store up hardship for old age.

[32] "'I am a companion of the gods, and a companion to good men. No noble deed, divine or mortal, takes place without me. I enjoy the greatest honour both among the gods and among men who are my kin. I am welcomed as a fellow worker by the artisan, I am a trusted guard for the master of the house, and a kindly protector to the slave; I am a good partner in the hard work of peace, a steady ally in the deeds of war, and the best companion in friendship. [33] And for my friends eating and drinking are pleasant and trouble-free; they simply hold off from doing so until they desire to. Their sleep is more enjoyable than that of those who do not work hard; they are not irritated when they must wake up nor do they neglect what needs to be done because they are sleepy. When they are young they enjoy the praise of their elders, and as old men they delight in the honour given them by the young. They take pleasure in remembering the deeds of their youth, and are pleased at the good deeds they do now; because of me they are dear to the gods, loved by their friends, and honoured by their fatherlands. And when their fated end comes, they do not lie without honour or forgotten, but live on forever in memory and in song. Such are the labours, O Heracles, thou son of goodly parents, that you can perform and thus acquire the most blessed happiness."

[34] 'This is what Prodicus said about the education of Heracles by Virtue, though he adorned these thoughts with language still grander than that I've used. You, then, Aristippus, should take this to heart and give some thought to your future life.'

1 Why does Vice/Happiness have two names, and Virtue only one?

2 On what grounds is the life offered by Virtue superior to that offered by Vice? Which life, ultimately, is more pleasant?

3 Why do you think Xenophon has Socrates cite Prodicus' story rather than arguing further with Aristippus? Which part of this chapter do you find more compelling, the argumentative first half, or the story of Heracles in the second?

4 How does Xenophon's treatment of these issues compare to things said to young people today? Have you been taught about the value of self-control? If so, how were you taught about this, and by whom? Was this teaching effective? Why or why not?

5 From what you know of Heracles' life in myth (or TV or film), did he follow Virtue's advice? If so, did her promises come true?

Self-control, addiction and intellectualism

Much of what we do is devoted to serving our desires. We recognize, of course, that sometimes our desires can get out of control, particularly regarding those things people can become addicted to: drugs such as alcohol, nicotine, and narcotics. And we sometimes speak of other forms of addiction – there are shopaholics, sex addicts, internet addicts, etc. Addiction is more a disease than a character flaw; it calls for treatment rather than (or at least in addition to) education. Addicts, for the most part, will not be able to moderate their desires: they must simply avoid the drug in question. But we tend to think that most people, most of the time, needn't worry about their desires; desires are natural and it is healthy for us to strive to fulfil them, so long as this doesn't lead to our making it difficult for others to fulfil their own desires.

In our Greek sources we find a rather different view. In this view, all people have to struggle against their desires in a constant pursuit of self-mastery. There is not some small class of desires, and objects of desire, that can lead to the problems we classify as addictions. Rather, all pleasures can be taken too far. And all people have to learn how to moderate their desires. Hence it is not surprising that Xenophon's Socrates makes so much of self-control (*enkrateia*), the ability to master one's desires.

But Socrates was also famous for saying that if one knows the right thing to do, one does it. This paradoxical claim is at the heart of what is known as Socratic intellectualism, the belief that knowledge is enough to allow one to make the right choices and lead the right sort of life. And 'the right thing' is both the just thing and the thing that is in one's own self-interest. Plato's Socrates almost never mentions self-control: if knowledge is enough, we don't need any strength of character to withstand temptation. Xenophon's Socrates puts far more emphasis on strength of character, but he also believes that knowledge suffices, and is incompatible with the absence of self-control.

> Asked if he thought that those who know what they should do but do the opposite are wise and lacking in self-control, he said, 'No more so than they are foolish and lacking self-control. For I think that all people choose, from the available options, what they think is most advantageous for them, and do it. So I hold that those who do not act correctly are neither wise nor moderate.' And he said that justice and all the rest of virtue was wisdom.
>
> (Xenophon, *Memorabilia* 3.9.5)

It is impossible to be wise and lack self-control. But if wisdom is sufficient, why make such a big deal out of self-control? Consider what Xenophon has Socrates say here:

> Doesn't it seem to you that a lack of self-control, by keeping wisdom, the greatest good, from men, pushes them in the opposite direction? Don't you think that it hinders people from paying attention to what is profitable and from fully understanding what that is, and drags them off towards what is pleasant? Often, after stunning those who perceive good things and bad ones, doesn't it make them choose the worse in place of the better?
>
> (Xenophon, *Memorabilia* 4.5.6)

- Can you come up with an example drawn from daily life that illustrates the point Xenophon's Socrates makes in that last paragraph? How can an absence of self-control undermine wisdom?

- So are our desires healthy natural urges we ought to act on, or is desire a force we must master so that it does not lead us astray?

The dancing Socrates

Socrates visiting Aspasia, *1842, engraving by Honoré Daumier.*

The French artist and caricaturist Honoré Daumier (1808–79) poked fun at figures of antiquity much as he did at the people of his own day. His original engraving was accompanied by the following little bit of verse:

A lover of wine and young girls
After dinner Socrates abandons philosophy
And like the dockworkers with their lady friends
He dances a little cancan.

Here Daumier has Socrates do a little dance for **Aspasia**, **Pericles**' controversial partner. As Aspasia (*c.* 470 to at least 428) was a citizen of Miletus, not Athens, Pericles could not marry her (thanks to a law he had passed himself!), but she was his *de facto* wife from around 450 until his death in 429. The Greek comic poets called her a *hetaira*, a high-class prostitute. Socratic sources, on the other hand, praise her, though the praise may be somewhat tongue in cheek. In Plato's *Menexenus*, Socrates rattles off a funeral oration he claims he was taught by Aspasia, and credits her with making Pericles the greatest Greek orator (235e). Xenophon's Socrates twice praises her ability at match-making or marriage counselling (*Memorabilia* 2.6.36 and *Oeconomicus* 3.14). While no Socratic source tells us of Socrates dancing for Aspasia, Xenophon does recount a visit Socrates made to another famous *hetaira*, Theodote, and has him coyly explain how she manages to earn gifts from her 'friends' (*Memorabilia* 3.13). And in his *Symposium* (3.16–19), Xenophon has Socrates explain to a shocked audience why he dances – something Greek aristocrats considered far beneath them: he does so to exercise his entire body at once. Certainly Socrates, whether he really danced for or learned from the likes of Aspasia, was no prude.

- Does the Socrates you encounter in this volume seem serious or playful? Would you invite him to a party?
- Do we expect wise men to dance with the likes of Aspasia?

5 Socrates and the sophists on ethics

Wisdom is the only good thing (Plato, *Euthydemus* 280b–281e)

We start this chapter with an excerpt from **Plato**'s *Euthydemus*. Socrates is reporting a conversation he had the day before with a young friend, Clinias, and two **sophists**, Euthydemus and Dionysodorus. The two sophists subject poor Clinias to a battery of tricky questions that no one can answer without contradicting himself. Socrates had asked the sophists to encourage Clinias to pursue philosophy; instead they show off their ability to humiliate him. Socrates, by contrast, delivers some of the clearest and most positive argumentation we find in early Plato; he does not merely find fault with positions of his **interlocutor** but argues to conclusions of his own. As we pick up the argument, Socrates has just argued that it is wisdom that makes one fortunate.

280b We concluded, at the end, somehow or other, that the gist of the matter was this: when wisdom was present, whoever had it had no additional need of good fortune.

And once we'd reached this conclusion, I asked him anew whether we still agreed to the things we had agreed on before.

'We agreed,' I said, 'that if we had **many good things**, we would be happy and do well.'

He agreed.

'Now does the presence of these goods make us happy if they benefit us, or if they don't benefit us?'

'If they benefit us,' he said.

280c 'And does something benefit us, if we merely have it, but don't use it? For example, if we have a great deal of food, but aren't eating it, or have something to drink, but aren't drinking it, would that benefit us?'

'Certainly not,' he said.

---

many good things Socrates and Clinias had agreed earlier that wealth, health, beauty, noble birth, power, honour, **virtue** and wisdom were good things.

'And what if a craftsman has acquired everything he needs to perform his work, but doesn't make use of what he's acquired? Would he do well just by having these things, because he has everything that a craftsman needs to have? Take a carpenter: if he had acquired all his tools and had plenty of wood, but didn't build anything, would he benefit from having these things?'

280d

'Not at all,' he said.

'What if someone had acquired money and all the goods we were talking about just now, but didn't use them? Would he be happy because he had those goods?'

'Certainly not, Socrates.'

'So it seems that it's not enough,' I said, 'just *to have* these sorts of goods, if one is going to be happy: one must also *use* them. Otherwise having them provides no benefit.'

'You're right.'

280e

'So, Clinias, it turns out that this is what it takes to make someone happy: both having good things and making use of them.'

'That's my view.'

'Is it when you use them correctly, or also when you don't use them correctly?'

'If you use them correctly.'

'Excellent,' I said. 'And if you aren't using something correctly, it makes a big difference whether you are actually making bad use of it, or just leave it alone. Using it will be bad, but if you don't use it the result will be neither good nor bad. Or do you disagree?'

281a

He agreed.

'Well, what then? Surely you agree that it is nothing other than the knowledge of carpentry that enables one to work with wood in the right way?'

'Certainly,' he said.

'And surely when one is working with one's tools it is also knowledge which enables one to do one's work correctly.'

He agreed.

'Now,' I said, 'when it comes to the goods we were talking about at first, wealth and health and beauty, is it knowledge that guides one to make the right use of these and makes one's actions correct, or something else?'

281b

'It is knowledge,' he said.

'So it seems that knowledge provides not only good fortune but success both in everything that people have and in everything that they do?'

He agreed.

'By Zeus,' I said, 'is any other possession worth anything if one lacks prudence and wisdom? Would anyone profit from owning many things and doing many things if he didn't have good sense – or would he profit more if he owned few things but was sensible? Here's how to look at it. Wouldn't someone who did less make fewer mistakes, and by making fewer mistakes wouldn't he do less badly, and by doing less badly wouldn't he be less miserable?'

281c

'Of course,' he said.

'Now would a poor man do less, or a rich one?'

'A poor one,' he said.

'A weak man or a strong one?'

'The weak one.'

'A man who is highly honoured, or one who is dishonoured?'

'The one who is dishonoured.'

'And does someone who is brave and moderate do less, or a coward?'

'The coward.'

'And a lazy man less than a hard-working one?'

He agreed.

281d

'And a slow one less than a fast one, and one with poor vision and hearing less than one with sharp senses?'

We agreed with each other on all such things.

'To sum it up, Clinias,' I said, 'our discussion of all those things we said were good has shown that they aren't naturally good in themselves. Instead, it looks like this. If ignorance is in control of such things, they are worse than their opposites, because they allow the person using them to get into more trouble. But if prudence and wisdom are in control, they are greater goods. By themselves, though, none of them is worth anything.'

281e

'It seems,' he said, 'that it does appear to be as you say.'

'So what can we conclude from what we've said? Isn't it that nothing else is either good or bad save for these two things, wisdom, which is good, and ignorance, which is bad?'

He agreed.

1 Why, according to Socrates, is it better for an ignorant person to be poor, ugly, half-blind and dishonoured?

2 Are all good things only good when we use them, as Socrates and Clinias agree? Or are there some things which you'd choose to have even if you never used them? And are there some good things that can't be used? How, for example, does one use a painting, or a spouse, or a child?

3 Are there perhaps some things so good that they can't be misused?

Socrates in the School of Athens

Detail from Raphael's School of Athens, *1511.*

Raphael is the first artist since antiquity to show knowledge of the ancient portrayal of Socrates. Most believe that it is Socrates who is depicted as the figure in green just left of centre in this section of Raphael's painting, and certainly his pug nose and imminent baldness match ancient versions, and his earnest conversational tone seems fitting. Many of the figures in Raphael's painting are, however, difficult to identify, and even Socrates' identity has been questioned of late. If he is Socrates, the armoured figure to the left ought to be **Alcibiades** (though others identify him as Alexander the Great). But the other figures in the Socrates group have not been safely identified. The two central figures in the painting, at the right of this image, are clearly enough labelled by Raphael: Plato holds his *Timaeus* and is pointing skyward, while the more down-to-earth **Aristotle** holds his *Ethics*.

- If you had to select a group of figures to illustrate the power of human reason today, who would you choose?

The powerless tyrant (Plato, *Gorgias* 466a–468e)

If virtue consists of knowledge, and this knowledge allows one to lead the best life, the next question is the object of this knowledge. Just what does one need to know to be virtuous? Knowledge of the good? But what is the good? In one Platonic dialogue, the *Protagoras*, Socrates appears to suggest that pleasure is the good, and that to lead a good life one needs to understand how to maximize one's pleasure over the entire course of one's life. That is, Socrates appears to endorse a form of **hedonism**. But elsewhere Socrates insists that the knowledge required for a good life isn't knowledge of pleasure, but rather has some moral content, as shown most clearly in his emphasis on the virtue of justice.

This emphasis on justice is clear in Plato's *Gorgias*, where Socrates debates with three difficult interlocutors on questions about the power of public speaking and the ethics of power. The title character, **Gorgias** (*c.* 485–*c.* 380 BC), was a citizen of Leontini, a Greek city in Sicily, and the most famous teacher of rhetoric in his day. Socrates confronts Gorgias with the problem of whether or not he is responsible if his students make unjust use of the rhetorical training he has provided them. After first implying that teachers should not be held responsible for students who misuse their training, Gorgias is ultimately shamed into agreeing that he would in the future teach justice to those of his students who lack it. At this point Polus, a protégé of Gorgias from Acragas (another Greek city in Sicily) takes over the conversation. Socrates first argues that rhetoric is not a true art or form of expertise (*technē*), but merely a knack for flattering your audience, a way to please them by telling them what they want to hear. Polus, rising to the defence of his craft, argues that skilled public speakers are the most powerful members of their societies. Our last three sections come from Plato's *Gorgias*, and carry the argument forward by discussing the nature of the wisdom Socrates has just recommended.

466a	POLUS	So what are you claiming? Do you think that rhetoric is flattery?
	SOCRATES	I actually said that it was *one sort* of flattery. You don't remember that, **Polus, at your age**? What are you going to do when you get old?
	POLUS	So do you think that the good orators are considered worthless in their cities because they are flatterers?
466b	SOCRATES	Are you asking a question, or beginning a speech?
	POLUS	I'm asking a question.
	SOCRATES	I don't think they're given any consideration at all.

Polus, at your age   Polus had already written at least one rhetorical treatise at the time of our conversation, but he was young enough to be the son of Socrates or Gorgias. His name means 'colt' in Greek, which adds to his rather juvenile persona here; earlier in the dialogue (at 463e), Socrates jokes that Polus is likely to bolt.

	POLUS	What do you mean, they're not given any consideration? Don't they have the greatest power in cities?
	SOCRATES	No, not if you say that having power is something good for the one with power.
	POLUS	But of course I say that!
	SOCRATES	I think that orators have the least power of anyone in the city.
466c	POLUS	What? Don't they, like tyrants, kill whomever they want to, and confiscate property and exile citizens from their cities as they think best?
	SOCRATES	**By the dog**, I really can't tell, Polus, whether you're speaking for yourself and revealing your own view each time you speak or if you are asking me a question.
	POLUS	No, I'm asking you a question.
	SOCRATES	All right, my friend. In that case, are you asking me two things at once?
	POLUS	How is it two things?
	SOCRATES	Didn't you say something like this: 'Don't the orators, like tyrants,
466d		kill whomever they want to, and confiscate property and exile citizens from their cities as they think best?'
	POLUS	I did.
	SOCRATES	Well, I say to you that there are two questions here, and I'll give you an answer to each. I maintain, Polus, that both orators and tyrants have the least power in cities, as I was saying just now. For they can
466e		do essentially nothing of *what they want to do*, **though they can do *what they think best*.**
	POLUS	Isn't that having great power?

By the dog   on this droll oath see the note at *Apology* **22a** (p. 40).

what they want to do, **though they can do *what they think best***   the distinction Socrates draws here isn't immediately clear, as Polus' confusion indicates. Socrates is arguing that people often fail to do what they truly want to do, not because some external force prevents them from doing it, but because they mistakenly choose to do something that they think is best, even though it isn't in fact best. Thus it is quite possible, in Socrates' view, to be mistaken about what one really wants. A tyrant can kill whomever he wants to kill, but unless he knows when this is in fact the best thing to do, this power is worthless.

So what do we really want? Our truest desire, Socrates implies, is for what is truly good, what is truly in our best interest. And while Socrates can't clearly define what this true good is, he does appear to assume that there is some objective answer to the question of what people really want. Today, on the other hand, we tend to assume that most people know what they want, and that individual people may well want very different things. And while there are some people who don't know what they really want, they need psychologists to help them plumb their inner selves, not a philosopher to teach them about the human good.

	SOCRATES	No, not according to Polus.
	POLUS	Not according to me? I say it is!
	SOCRATES	No, I swear you don't, since you said that having power is good for the person who has it.
	POLUS	That is my position.
	SOCRATES	Do you believe that it is a good thing if someone does what he thinks best, but lacks any **insight**? Do you call this having great power?
	POLUS	I don't.
467a	SOCRATES	So are you going to prove that orators have insight and that rhetoric is an art, and not mere flattery, and thus refute me? If you let me off without refuting me, the orators who do what they think is best in their cities, just as tyrants do, will not have done themselves any good. And power, as you say, is a good thing, while you yourself agree that doing what one thinks best isn't good, if one doesn't have any insight into the matter. Right?
	POLUS	Yes.
	SOCRATES	So how do orators or tyrants have great power in their cities, unless Polus refutes Socrates and shows that they actually do what they want to do?
467b	POLUS	What is this fellow up to?
	SOCRATES	I deny that they do what they want to do. Now refute me.
	POLUS	Didn't you just agree that they do whatever they think best?
	SOCRATES	Yes, and I agree with that still.
	POLUS	But don't they do what they want to do?
	SOCRATES	No, I say they don't.
	POLUS	While they're doing what they think best?
	SOCRATES	That's what I say.
	POLUS	This is outrageous and bizarre talk, Socrates!
467c	SOCRATES	Don't attack me, my potent Polus – to address you **in your own fashion**. If you've got a question to ask me, show that I'm wrong. Otherwise, answer the questions yourself.
	POLUS	Well, I'm willing to answer in order to find out what you're talking about.

insight Socrates has argued (in a portion of the dialogue not given in this text) that orators do not have any knowledge about their subject-matter. Hence their skill in public speaking allows them to get things done (by persuading the **Assembly** to pass a measure they have proposed, for example); but this doesn't give them any insight into what they ought to be doing.

in your own fashion Polus as a rhetorician, especially as one who was a fan of Gorgias, would have been fond of the sound effects in phrases like 'potent Polus' (*ō lōiste Pōle* in Greek); excessive fondness of word-play was called 'Gorgianic' in antiquity.

Socrates false and true

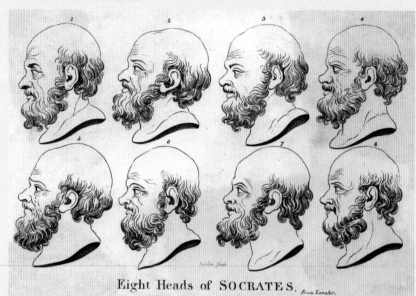

Faulty renderings of Socrates.

Drawing, at several removes, of a lost bust of Socrates.

Socrates was one of the first case-studies in the art of physiognomy, whose practitioners believed that they could identify a person's character through his or her appearance. The story apparently goes back to a now-lost dialogue by Socrates' companion Phaedo; the relevant passage is preserved for us by **Cicero**:

When Zopyrus, who claimed that he could recognize each man's nature from his appearance, said in a public meeting that he had found many vices in Socrates, all the rest laughed at him, since they did not recognize those vices in Socrates. But Socrates himself supported Zopyrus, since he said that he had been born with these vices, but had removed them by means of reason.

(Cicero, *Tusculan Disputations* 4.80)

In another passage, Cicero notes that Alcibiades laughed out loud when Zopyrus reported that Socrates was not only stupid and dull but a womanizer (*On Fate* 5.10). The contrast between Socrates' ugly appearance and his beautiful **soul** continued to challenge later physiognomists. Most argued that Socrates' ability to overcome his innate flaws showed the power of rationality, or perhaps of divine grace. But the last great physiognomist, John Caspar Lavater (1741–1801), argued that many ancient artists had missed Socrates' true appearance, which actually revealed his true character to those with the skill to recognize it. Lavater concluded that Socrates must have looked like an engraving (opposite) of a lost drawing by Peter Paul Rubens which was based on a lost portrait bust that may or may not have ever represented Socrates in the first place! Perhaps this bust resembled that pictured on p. 75, at least if we can trust the depiction of the eyes in this engraving.

Lavater also illustrated eight different ways artists could get Socrates' features wrong. To this day, as we have seen (pp. 9–10), scholars divide portraits of Socrates into two camps, those looking more like a **satyr** (**type A**) and those looking less like a satyr, which attempt to reveal Socrates' inner character (**type B**). Thus we, just like the physiognomists of old, are still trying to see whether inner character is reflected in facial features.

- Can you characterize how the 'true Socrates' differs from the faulty representations of him?

SOCRATES   Do you think that people want *whatever it is they are doing* at the time, or want *the objective for which* they are doing something? Take people who are getting medicine from doctors. Do you think that they want to do what they are doing – to drink the foul-tasting medicine – or want to be healthy, their objective in drinking it?

POLUS   Clearly they want to be healthy.

467d   SOCRATES   And those who **go to sea in pursuit of trade**, or engage in trade in some other way, don't do what they want to as they do this – for who wants to face danger at sea and take all that trouble? But they do, I think, want wealth, which is their objective when they go to sea. For it's for the sake of wealth that they go to sea.

POLUS   Of course.

go to sea in pursuit of trade   given the difficult terrain and poor roads, transport by land was often prohibitively expensive in ancient Greece, so most traders went by sea and hence risked their cargoes and even their lives.

	SOCRATES	So does the same hold in all cases? Whenever someone does something for the sake of something else, he doesn't want the thing he's doing, does he, but the objective for which he's doing it?
	POLUS	Yes.
467e	SOCRATES	Now does anything exist which is neither good nor bad nor intermediate between these, neither good nor bad?
	POLUS	There can't be any such thing, Socrates.
	SOCRATES	And do you say that **wisdom and health and wealth and other things of this sort are good**, while their opposites are bad?
	POLUS	I do.
468a	SOCRATES	And is this the sort of thing you mean by things that are neither good nor bad: things which sometimes share in something good, sometimes share in something bad, and sometimes in neither, like sitting and walking and running and sailing, or like stones and wood and other things like that? Isn't that what you mean? Or are there other things which you say are neither good nor bad?
	POLUS	No, that's what I mean.
	SOCRATES	So whenever people do something, do they do the neutral things for the sake of the good ones, or the good ones for the sake of the neutral ones?
468b	POLUS	They do the neutral things for the sake of the good ones.
	SOCRATES	So whenever we walk, we do so in pursuit of what's good, because we believe it is better to do so? And in the opposite case, whenever we stand still, we do it for the same reason, the good. Right?
	POLUS	Yes.
	SOCRATES	So we kill, if we kill someone, and exile people and confiscate property when we believe that it is better for us to do so than not to?
	POLUS	Of course.
	SOCRATES	So whenever someone is doing anything, he does it for the sake of the good?
	POLUS	I say so.
468c	SOCRATES	And we agreed that we don't want the things we are doing, but the objectives for which we do something.
	POLUS	Absolutely.

---

wisdom and health and wealth and other things of this sort are good   this contradicts the conclusion reached in the *Euthydemus*, as we saw above, where Socrates denied that anything other than wisdom was good. But here Socrates may simply adopt the common belief that things like health and wealth are good, rather than vouching for the goodness of such things himself.

	SOCRATES	So we don't want to slaughter people or exile them from the city or take their money just like that; rather we want to do it *if it is advantageous for us*, as you maintain; and we don't want what is neither good nor bad, nor do we want what is bad. Isn't that right? Do you think that what I'm saying is true, Polus, or not? Why don't you answer?
	POLUS	It's true.
468d	SOCRATES	Since we agree about that, if someone, whether a tyrant or an orator, kills people, or exiles them or takes their property, believing that it is best for him, but it actually is bad for him, then this person does indeed do *what he thinks best*. Isn't that right?
	POLUS	Yes.
	SOCRATES	So does he also do *what he wants to*, if these things are actually bad? Why don't you answer?
	POLUS	No, I don't think he does what he wants to do.
468e	SOCRATES	So is there any way that such a person could have great power in his city, if having great power is something good, as you agree?
	POLUS	There isn't.
	SOCRATES	So I was right, then, when I said that it is possible for someone who does what he thinks best in a city neither to have great power nor to do what he wants to do?

1 Try to say in your own words what Socrates means by the following paradoxical claims. Then try to say why he believes these claims are true.

   An absolute tyrant may have no power at all.

   People often don't want to do what they're doing, even if they think it's the best thing to do.

2 What would true power be, for Socrates?

3 Socrates implies that we often mistake means for ends, that we think we want one thing, when what we really want is some more distant objective. This sometimes leads us to pursue means and forget about ends, as Polus seems to pursue political influence without giving any thought to what such influence should be used for. Is this true to your experience? That is, have you found yourself pursuing something only to forget why you wanted it in the first place?

Another death of Socrates

The Death of Socrates, *1762, by Jacques-Philip-Joseph de Saint-Quentin. (Black and white photo of colour original.)*

The French Académie des Beaux Arts held a prestigious artistic competition each year, and 1762 was the first year the Academy chose a theme from classical antiquity rather than from the Bible. The death of Socrates was the theme chosen, and Saint-Quentin's painting won the competition. His version differs tremendously from the more famous picture by David, which was produced just 25 years later. Here Socrates reels as the poison hits home, though he still has the strength to hold back the distraught figure above him. Two other followers, their arms clasped as if in prayer, react emotionally to the scene. We have, as in Carracci's version of 'Hercules at the Crossroads' (p. 117), a figure taking notes; compare also David's Plato, though David's figure has dropped his scroll.

- Compare this painting with David's more famous image on p. 26. How would you describe the differences between the two? Which do you like better, and why?

- Why is the death of Socrates such an iconic scene? Which scene (or scenes) from the Bible have reached similar status? What scenes from the history of your country are iconic? Are there any features common to all such scenes?

Callicles challenges Socrates (Plato, *Gorgias* 482c–491e)

In the next section of Plato's *Gorgias*, Socrates goes on to try to convince Polus that practical power of the sort he desires is only valuable when used justly, and that justice is always preferable to injustice. In fact, it is far better to suffer from injustice than to commit it, Socrates claims; and if you have done wrong, you are better off getting punished, as this will make you more just and hence happier. Socrates now draws the paradoxical conclusion that skill in public speaking is only valuable for two things: if you are guilty, you can use it to convince a court to inflict punishment on yourself, as this would make you more just and hence less miserable; or, if your enemy is guilty, you can use it to convince a court not to punish him, as punishment would make him less miserable!

This is too much for Callicles, Socrates' next interlocutor, a still more radical figure than Polus. Callicles was not an out-of-town teacher of rhetoric like Gorgias and Polus but an Athenian who longed for political power. Given that he appears nowhere else in our historical record, Callicles apparently did not get the power he wanted; perhaps his radical views were his undoing. Callicles would overturn the popular morality based on human convention, and seems to see himself as something of a Nietzschean *Übermensch* (superhuman) whose natural superiority ought to be given free rein.

482c	CALLICLES	Socrates, you've spoken with the abandon of youth, **like a true demagogue**; and just now you can play the demagogue because Polus has suffered the same fate that he said you inflicted on Gorgias. **At one point** Polus said that Gorgias was ashamed when you asked what he would do if someone who wanted to study rhetoric came to him without any knowledge of justice. When you asked whether he'd teach him justice, Gorgias agreed that he would teach him, answering as people normally do to avoid getting others upset when one doesn't agree with them. And this concession forced Gorgias to contradict himself, your very favourite thing. At that point Polus laughed at you – and rightly so, I think. But now the same thing has happened to him. And for the very same reason I don't admire Polus: he conceded

482d

---

like a true demagogue   Callicles thus charges Socrates with speaking like a popular politician – throwing back at Socrates his own claim that it was Gorgias and Polus who spoke in this way, while Socrates sought only the truth.

At one point   *Gorgias* 461b–c.

483b

483a

482e

to you that it is **more shameful to do injustice than to suffer it.** Thanks to this agreement he was tripped up and found himself tongue-tied during the argument, because he was ashamed to say what he thought.

In reality, Socrates, though you say you are pursuing the truth, you trot out cheap platitudes like these, things which **aren't admirable by nature, but by custom.** For the most part these things, nature and custom, are opposed to one another. So if someone is ashamed and doesn't dare to say what he thinks, he's forced to contradict himself. You've figured out this clever trick and cheat with it when you argue. Whenever someone is speaking of what's customary, you slyly ask him about what's natural, and when someone speaks of what's natural, you ask about custom. This is just what you did just now, concerning justice and injustice. When Polus spoke in conventional terms and said that doing injustice was more shameful than suffering it, you went after his argument in terms of what is natural. For by nature everything that is worse is more shameful, including suffering injustice; it's by custom that doing injustice is more shameful. Suffering injustice isn't for real men but for **slaves,** people better off

---

more shameful to do injustice than to suffer it Polus attempted to argue that while it was more shameful to do injustice than to suffer it, it was better to do it than to suffer it. But Socrates forced him to agree that doing injustice was not only more shameful but worse (*Gorgias* 474c–475c).

aren't admirable by nature, but by custom the Greek terms are *physis* (nature) and *nomos* (which can mean custom, convention or law); the opposition between the two was a key theme in the debates of Socrates' day (see pp. 16–17). Callicles, as we shall see, champions *physis* over *nomos*, what is natural over what is merely an artificial human construct. In his view *physis* calls for a distinctly troubling ethical theory, one in which the strong ought to prey on the weak by running society in their own selfish interest, regardless of what is in the best interest of others.

slaves Callicles, consistently enough, speaks here of people who are slaves by nature, because they are incapable of looking after themselves. Some Greek thinkers doubted whether slavery as practised in the Greek world had a natural basis. If it was merely human convention that determined who was slave and who was free, then slavery could be unnatural and unjust. Aristotle defended slavery by arguing that some people are, by nature, better off as slaves, because they lack the mental capacity to manage their own lives (*Politics* 1.2.1254a17–1255b16). While none of our sources show Socrates directly addressing the question of slavery, we have no good reason to believe that he would have come to a different conclusion from Aristotle. Most slaves in the Greek world were non-Greek, and most Greeks assumed that non-Greeks (barbarians) were, by nature, better suited to be slaves.

dead than alive, who can help neither themselves nor anyone they care for when they suffer injustice and are treated like dirt.

No, I think that the ones who set up the **laws** are the weak people, the majority. So they set up laws that are advantageous to themselves, and direct their praise and blame accordingly. They're terrified of the strongest people, who are capable of getting more. To prevent them from getting more than they get, they say that it's shameful and unjust to get more than others do, and that this is what injustice is, getting more than others. For they themselves, I think, are pleased if they can get **an equal share**, since they are so worthless themselves. This is why it's customary to say that it is unjust and shameful to have more than most people, and most people call this doing injustice. But nature herself, I believe, reveals that it is just that the better have more than the worse and that the more capable have more than the less capable.

483c

483d

Socrates now proceeds to quiz Callicles on what he means by 'better' and 'more capable' and what he thinks such people should have more of. We skip a few pages of the *Gorgias* and rejoin it at the last stage of this argument.

---

laws   the Greek is *nomoi*, the plural of *nomos*, the same term translated as 'custom' above. While social customs will reflect the beliefs of the majority in any society, Callicles' argument will apply with greatest force to a democracy like Athens, where it is indeed the majority who elevate such customs to the status of laws. Callicles presumably sees himself as a natural tyrant, who ought to be able to set up society to serve his own interest. Defenders of Athenian democracy, on the other hand, would have defended their laws as a sort of social contract, pulling them out of the nasty and brutish state of nature Callicles describes. Socrates describes another sort of social contract – not that of original citizens forming the state, but of contemporary citizens with the laws of their states – in Plato's *Crito*. This line of thought would be developed further by modern thinkers such as Thomas Hobbes (1588–1679), John Locke (1632–1704) and Jean-Jacques Rousseau (1712–78).

an equal share   equality was a fundamental value in Greek political thinking, as in much modern political thought. When the Athenians developed their democratic institutions in 507 BC, democrats made *isonomia*, 'equality before the law', one of their prime slogans. And under the democracy, all Athenian citizens had an equal opportunity to shape the formation of Athenian law (in the Assembly) and to enforce it (as litigants and as members of the jury in Athenian courts). *Isonomia* was a less controversial term than *dēmokratia*, which could imply rule of the poor over the rich. Callicles, however, is hostile even to *isonomia*: in his view only the strong should rule.

491c	SOCRATES	But, my good fellow, say once and for all who you mean by 'the better' and 'the stronger' and what they are better and stronger at.
491d	CALLICLES	But I have already said that it is those who understand how to run the city and are brave. It's these people who should rule cities, and what's just is that they have more than the other people, the rulers more than the ruled.
	SOCRATES	And what about their relationship with themselves?
	CALLICLES	What are you talking about?
	SOCRATES	Are they rulers or ruled?
	CALLICLES	What do you mean?
	SOCRATES	I'm talking about each one ruling himself. Or is ruling oneself not required, just ruling others?
	CALLICLES	What do you mean by ruling oneself?
491e	SOCRATES	Nothing fancy, just what most people mean, **being moderate and having control over oneself** by ruling the pleasures and desires in oneself.
	CALLICLES	What a sweetheart you are! When you say 'moderate' you mean 'stupid'.
	SOCRATES	What? Anyone can see that that's not what I'm saying.
	CALLICLES	It obviously *is* what you're saying, Socrates. For how could a person be happy if he is enslaved to anyone? No, I'll tell you now very frankly what is admirable and just by nature. Here's the correct way to live your life: you must allow your desires to grow as great as possible and not check them, and when they get as great as possible you must be able to serve them through courage and intelligence, and always get whatever you desire.

1 Would you agree with Callicles that laws are passed to protect the majority, but perhaps needn't apply to exceptional people? Aren't we sometimes tempted to allow some people greater licence than others?

2 Does Callicles' brand of hedonism differ from that advocated by **Aristippus** in **Xenophon** (in chapter 4)? If so, how?

3 Would Callicles, who clearly sees himself as a potential leader of the city, thanks to his intelligence and courage, be susceptible to the sorts of argument Xenophon's Socrates made to Aristippus in chapter 4?

4 Do you think that Socrates sees any meaningful distinction between *physis* and *nomos* (nature and custom)?

5 Do you prefer what is natural to what is artificial? Why or why not?

---

being moderate and having control over oneself self-control is one of the major concerns of Xenophon's Socrates, as we saw in chapter 4.

Socrates rescues Alcibiades

Socrates tears Alcibiades away from the embrace of pleasure, *1791, by Jean-Baptiste Regnault.*

Regnault, a contemporary and sometime rival of Jacques-Louis David (see the illustration on p. 26), portrays Socrates as an outraged mentor saving Alcibiades from the charms of beautiful women companions. There is no ancient textual evidence for any such scene. The closest thing in our ancient sources is a rather different episode, Alcibiades' failed attempt to seduce Socrates. As Alcibiades tells the tale in Plato's *Symposium*, he arranged to be all alone with Socrates one night, and offered Socrates a deal: Alcibiades would trade his own considerable beauty (that is, have sex with Socrates) in exchange for Socrates' wisdom. Socrates dryly responded that if he indeed was wise, this would be a good bargain for Alcibiades, who would be trading mere physical beauty for beauty of the soul, beauty of a far greater sort. He warned Alcibiades, though, that he might not have any wisdom after all – in which case Alcibiades would be making a bad deal. Here's what Alcibiades says next:

I thought, after I'd said that and heard what he'd said, having shot my bolt, so to speak, that I'd hit the mark. So I got up, didn't allow him to say another word, put this cloak of mine around his threadbare robe (it was winter), lay down beside him, and threw my arms around this wonderfully divine man. I lay there the whole night long – and here, Socrates, you can't say that I'm lying. But when I did this he was so superior to my beauty – precisely where I thought I was really something, gentlemen of the jury (for you are sitting in judgement on Socrates' arrogance) – he was so contemptuous and mocking, so hubristic, that, I assure you, by the gods, by the goddesses, I slept through that night and woke up next to Socrates just as I had slept beside my father or an elder brother.

(Plato, *Symposium* 219b–c)

- Is the figure described here by Alcibiades the same Socrates whom Regnault depicts angrily dragging Alcibiades from a den of iniquity?

Socrates refutes Callicles (Plato, *Gorgias* 497e–499b)

Socrates, however, rejects Callicles' view. He compares the life Callicles praises to that of a foul bird that eats and excretes all day, or a man with unseemly and insatiable sexual desires. Callicles retorts that Socrates would praise the static life of a stone or corpse, of people so self-controlled that they desire nothing. Here we consider one of Socrates' arguments meant to show that pleasure cannot be the only goal worth pursuing.

497e   SOCRATES   If you'd like, look at it like this, since I don't think you agree with **that argument**. But do look at it like this. Don't you call good people **good because of the presence of good things**, just as you call people noble because of the nobility present in them?

       CALLICLES   I do.

---

that argument   Socrates has just argued (at *Gorgias* 495e–497d) that while one does not possess a good thing and its opposite at the same time, one does feel pleasure and pain at the same time, as when one drinks while thirsty. So pleasure can't be the good. Callicles has grudgingly gone along with the argument, but Socrates recognizes that he doesn't buy it.

good because of the presence of good things   is just as vague in the Greek as in this English, and the same holds for Socrates' claim that we call people noble (or admirable or fine or beautiful, all translations of the Greek *kalos*) because of some nobility present in them. Callicles argues that pleasure is the good, so the things that make people good will be pleasures. But he also retains the idea that brave and intelligent people are good. Socrates will use this ambiguity in Callicles' understanding of the good to trip him up.

	SOCRATES	And do you call foolish and cowardly men good? Just now you didn't, but rather those who are brave and intelligent. Isn't it these you call good?
	CALLICLES	Absolutely.
	SOCRATES	And have you ever seen a thoughtless child enjoying himself?
	CALLICLES	I have.
	SOCRATES	And have you never seen a thoughtless man enjoying himself?
	CALLICLES	I think I have, but what of it?
498a	SOCRATES	Oh, nothing, just answer me.
	CALLICLES	Yes, I have seen that.
	SOCRATES	And you've seen a sensible man in pain and seen him enjoying himself?
	CALLICLES	Yes.
	SOCRATES	Which enjoy themselves more and feel more pain, the intelligent or the foolish?
	CALLICLES	I don't think there's much difference.
	SOCRATES	Okay, that's close enough. Have you ever seen a cowardly man at war?
	CALLICLES	Of course.
	SOCRATES	Well, what of this: when the enemy departed, which seemed to you to enjoy this more, the cowards or the brave?
498b	CALLICLES	Both, I think; either the cowards enjoyed it more or both enjoyed it more or less the same amount.
	SOCRATES	That doesn't make any difference. So cowards do enjoy things?
	CALLICLES	Very much so.
	SOCRATES	As do fools, it seems.
	CALLICLES	Yes.
	SOCRATES	And when the enemy approaches, is it only the cowards who feel pain, or the brave men too?
	CALLICLES	Both.
	SOCRATES	To the same degree?
	CALLICLES	Perhaps the cowards a bit more.
	SOCRATES	And when the enemy departs they enjoy it more?
	CALLICLES	Perhaps.
	SOCRATES	So pain and joy are experienced by both fools and intelligent men alike, and by both cowards and the brave, as you say, and the cowards
498c		experience even more of this than the brave?
	CALLICLES	That's what I say.
	SOCRATES	Now the intelligent and the brave are good, while the cowardly and foolish are bad?
	CALLICLES	Yes.
	SOCRATES	So good men and bad ones enjoy themselves and feel pain to about the same extent?
	CALLICLES	I'd say so.

	SOCRATES	So are both good men and bad ones good and bad to pretty much the same degree? Or are the bad even better?
498d	CALLICLES	By Zeus, I don't know what you mean.
	SOCRATES	Don't you understand that you say that the good are good through the presence of good things, and the bad through the presence of bad ones? And what's good is pleasure, while what's bad is pain?
	CALLICLES	I do.
	SOCRATES	So those who are enjoying themselves have good things, pleasures, if they are indeed enjoying themselves?
	CALLICLES	Of course.
	SOCRATES	So those who are enjoying themselves are good because good things are present?
	CALLICLES	Yes.
	SOCRATES	Well, aren't bad things, pains, present for those who are in distress?
	CALLICLES	They are.
498e	SOCRATES	And you say that bad men are bad through the presence of bad things? Or don't you say that any more?
	CALLICLES	I do say that.
	SOCRATES	So those who are enjoying themselves are good, while those who are distressed are bad?
	CALLICLES	Certainly.
	SOCRATES	And the more they enjoy themselves, the better they are, and the more they are in distress, the worse they are, while those who experience less of these things are less good or bad, and those who experience them to about the same degree are good or bad in about the same degree?
	CALLICLES	Yes.
	SOCRATES	So you're saying that the intelligent and foolish and the cowardly and brave enjoy themselves and feel pain to about the same degree, or the cowardly do so to an even greater degree?
	CALLICLES	Yes.
499a	SOCRATES	Join me in seeing what follows from the things we've agreed to. As the saying goes, ''tis fine twice and even thrice' to say and study what is fine. We say that the intelligent and brave man is good. Right?
	CALLICLES	Right.
	SOCRATES	And the foolish and cowardly one is bad.
	CALLICLES	Quite so.
	SOCRATES	And one who is enjoying himself is good?
	CALLICLES	Yes.
	SOCRATES	And one in distress is bad?
	CALLICLES	Necessarily.

SOCRATES	And good and bad men are distressed and enjoy themselves in the same way, or perhaps the bad man experiences this even more?
CALLICLES	Yes.
SOCRATES	So the bad man becomes just as good and bad as the good one does, or perhaps becomes even more good than the good man does?

499b

	Doesn't this follow, **like that earlier conclusion**, whenever one says that what's good is the same thing as what's pleasant?
CALLICLES	You know, I've been listening to you for a long time, Socrates, agreeing all along, and thinking that even if someone grants you something in jest, you're delighted with it and seize on it like a child would. As if you believed that I, or any other person in the world, didn't believe that some pleasures are better than others.

Callicles has been refuted by a Socratic **elenchus** (see the text box on pp. 93–4). We can sketch it like this:

1 Brave and intelligent men are good, and cowards and fools are bad (*Gorgias* 491b–c, not quoted above; this reflects the conventional belief that some men are superior to others, and more virtuous than them).

2 But cowards and fools get at least as much pleasure as brave and intelligent men (what Socrates gets Callicles to agree to in the argument above).

3 The presence of pleasure makes a man good, and the presence of pain makes him bad (*Gorgias* **498e**, quoted just above: Callicles' hedonism).

4 But this means that bad men (cowards and fools) are at least as good as good men (brave and intelligent men) because they experience at least as much pleasure. Which is absurd.

Callicles, in this respect at least like the usual Socratic interlocutor, abandons the premise Socrates disagrees with. By saying that he thinks that some pleasures are better than others, he must abandon (or at least radically modify) step 3, and hence abandon his hard-core hedonism. For it will not only be pleasure which makes life good, but whatever it is that makes some pleasures better than others. Socrates goes on to lead an increasingly sullen Callicles through more arguments meant to show the superiority of the virtuous and moderate life, and closes the *Gorgias* with a powerful myth explaining the different fates awaiting the virtuous and villainous in the afterlife.

like that earlier conclusion   Socrates probably refers to the argument which concluded at *Gorgias* 494e, where he forced Callicles to say that the most shameful pleasures were good.

1 Do you believe, as Socrates argues here, that people who are intelligent and brave enjoy no more pleasure than those who are foolish and cowardly? Why or why not? If you disagree with Socrates, how would you have helped Callicles to avoid losing this argument?

2 Callicles argued (**482c–e**, pp. 139–40) that Gorgias and Polus were refuted because they were too embarrassed to stand by their unconventional principles. When push came to shove, they resorted to talking in conventional terms (according to *nomos*) rather than sticking to the philosophically sounder ground of nature (*physis*). Is this also Callicles' downfall? That is, does he lose the argument because he resorts to conventional terms in calling the intelligent and brave good? Or does Socrates reveal a deep contradiction between Callicles' hedonism and his belief that some men (like Callicles himself) are superior beings?

3 Why does Socrates choose to argue with the likes of Callicles? Is arguing with someone who disagrees vehemently with you a good way to improve your own thinking? Why or why not?

4 Now that we've reached the end of our introduction to Socrates, take a stab at summing up what Socrates can teach us about his favourite question. What makes for a good life? Virtue? Power? Pleasure? Wisdom? What have you learned from Socrates?

Socrates gets drenched

Xanthippe Dousing Socrates, c. *1655, by Reyer van Blommendael (previously attributed to Cesar van Everdingen).*

Socrates and his wife – or wives – provided comic material for later writers and artists. Socrates' wife, Xanthippe, was said to be a shrew. Xenophon gives us some early evidence for this view, as he relates how Socrates counselled his son to deal with his mother's scolding (*Memorabilia* 2.2) and has **Antisthenes** question why Socrates chose to marry such a difficult woman (*Symposium* 2.10).

The story of Xanthippe dumping water on Socrates is found only later (as in **Diogenes Laertius** 2.17), but became quite popular in the Renaissance, when it was employed to illustrate the virtue of patience. Various ancient sources say that Socrates had two wives (see Diogenes Laertius 2.26), the second being Myrto, granddaughter of the famous Athenian statesman Aristides the Just. In some versions of the tale Socrates is married to both at once; in others he marries Myrto after the death of Xanthippe. The most plausible story is that Socrates took Myrto under his protection after the death of her husband. In any event, tales of a second wife (or mistress cohabitating with a wife) offered the chance to portray Socrates as a husband henpecked by both Xanthippe and Myrto.

In our painting Xanthippe teams up with Myrto and both glare at Socrates, their breasts belligerently bare, as if they would use them to douse him as well, if only they could. Getting an eyeful to the left is a young Alcibiades, suitably accompanied by an aristocratic hunting dog (in another ancient story, an older Alcibiades was said to have cut the tail off his dog to give people something to talk about and divert them from the rest of his outrageous behaviour). Here Socrates, barefoot, resting on a block that happens to be labelled 'Know Thyself' in Greek, appears utterly relaxed, and may even wear something of a leer. He is not so much the embodiment of virtuous patience as of an utter lack of concern for conventional values, including the concern to maintain a dignified household.

- Is there something particularly comical about a philosopher with a difficult marriage? And would such a marriage call his wisdom into question?

Further reading

Start with the primary sources. Plato's dialogues are readily accessible in the fine translations in *Plato: Complete Works,* edited by **John M. Cooper** (Indianapolis, 1997). Xenophon's Socratic works can be found in *Conversations of Socrates* edited by **Robin Waterfield** (London, 1990); Waterfield also provides an insightful introduction to Xenophon's Socratic works. One good recent translation of Aristophanes' *Clouds* is that of **Jeffery Henderson** (Newburyport, MA, 1992). Later sources on Socrates are conveniently gathered in *The Unknown Socrates,* edited by **William H. Calder** and others (Wauconda, IL, 2002). The texts of Socrates' sophistic rivals are helpfully translated by **Rosamund Kent Sprague** in *The Older Sophists* (Columbia, SC, 1972). For help with the cast of characters who appear with Socrates, **Debra Nails**' *The People of Plato* (Indianapolis, 2002) is invaluable, and not only for Plato.

For a fine and concise scholarly account of Socrates, see *Socrates: A Very Short Introduction* (Oxford, 1998) by **C. C. W. Taylor**. The third volume of **W. K. C. Guthrie**'s *A History of Greek Philosophy* (Cambridge, 1971) contains a comprehensive introduction to Socrates and the sophists, though it is now somewhat dated. **Gregory Vlastos**' vastly influential work on Socrates can best be approached via his *Socrates: Ironist and Moral Philosopher* (Ithaca, NY, 1991). Among those working in the tradition of Vlastos are **Thomas C. Brickhouse and Nicholas D. Smith**, who offer a fine introduction to the analytical approach to Socrates in *The Philosophy of Socrates* (Boulder, 2000). **Mark McPherran**, working in the same tradition, ably analyses Socrates' religion and is unusually open to the evidence from Xenophon (*The Religion of Socrates*, University Park, PA, 1996).

Recent volumes collecting articles on Socrates provide a good way to introduce yourself to the rich contemporary scholarship on him. The new *Cambridge Companion to Socrates*, edited by **Donald Morrison** (Cambridge, 2010), is an excellent place to start. The *Cambridge Companion to Plato*, edited by **Richard Kraut** (Cambridge, 1992), naturally contains much of interest on Socrates, as does the Blackwell *Companion to Plato*, edited by **Hugh Benson** (Oxford, 2006). The Blackwell *Companion to Socrates*, edited by **Sara Ahbel-Rappe and Rachana Kamtekar** (Oxford, 2006) is particularly strong on Socrates' legacy in Hellenistic philosophy and beyond. The Socratic legacy is the explicit target of two volumes edited by **Michael Trapp**, *Socrates from Antiquity to the Enlightenment* and *Socrates in the Nineteenth and Twentieth Centuries* (London, 2007).

Most scholarship on Plato and Socrates is in the analytical tradition, which aims to identify and analyse philosophical arguments worthy of our consideration. Work by Vlastos and those responding to him falls into this camp. The most prominent alternative approach is that of the conservative political philosopher **Leo Strauss** (1899–1973), which is most accessible in his 'Five Lectures on Socrates' in

The Rebirth of Classical Political Rationalism: An Introduction to the Thought of Leo Strauss, edited by **Thomas Pangle** (Chicago, 1989). Strauss argues that Plato and Xenophon, realizing that philosophy has no final answers to the largest questions, produced playful works of philosophical literature that articulate these questions and reveal why they can't be answered – or at least do so for readers able to 'read between the lines'.

For another alternative to the analytical approach, consider **Alexander Nehamas'** *The Art of Living: Socratic Reflections from Plato to Foucault* (Berkeley, 2000); Nehamas eloquently rejects the attempt to recover Socrates' original thought, and replaces it with an account of how Montaigne, Nietzsche and Foucault made use of Socrates to fashion their own philosophical identities. And for an approach that emphasizes literary qualities of Plato, consider **Ruby Blondell**, *The Play of Character in Plato's Dialogues* (Cambridge, 2002).

Socrates' trial has been the focus of considerable debate over the last 20 years. The muck-raking American journalist **I. F. Stone** learned Greek in his retirement and turned his journalistic skills to the case of Socrates; his best-selling *The Trial of Socrates* (New York, 1988) identified political motives behind that trial, but did so in a way many classicists have found somewhat suspect. In the next year two more scholarly books appeared, *Socrates on Trial*, by **Thomas Brickhouse and Nicholas D. Smith** (Oxford, 1989) and *Socrates in the* Apology: *An Essay on Plato's* Apology of Socrates (Indianapolis, 1989), by **C. D. C. Reeve**. Both of these argue that Plato's Socrates squarely faces the charges against him and that the political issues raised by Xenophon were not important in 399 BC. **Robin Waterfield**'s *Why Socrates Died: Dispelling the Myths* (New York, 2009) aims to restore the political context to the trial, and does so in a very accessible way. **Bettany Hughes'** new *The Hemlock Cup: Socrates, Athens and the Search for the Good Life* (London, 2010) similarly emphasizes Socrates' historical and cultural context, and provides a lively description of life in ancient Athens.

For scholarship on Socrates outside Plato, see **Paul Vander-Waerdt**'s *The Socratic Movement* (Ithaca, NY, 1994), which contains many essays on other sources, including Vander-Waerdt's own excellent essay on Socrates in the *Clouds*. For Xenophon, in addition to the essays in Vander-Waerdt, see **Louis-André Dorion**'s essay in the Blackwell *Companion to Socrates* (cited just above) and **Deborah Gera**'s essay in *Socrates from Antiquity to the Enlightenment* (also cited above). My own somewhat different approach to Xenophon's Socrates can be sampled in 'Xenophon's Socrates at his Most Socratic: *Memorabilia* 4.2' in the 2006 volume of *Oxford Studies in Ancient Philosophy*.

Socrates' many appearances in ancient and modern art have been much studied of late. **Paul Zanker**'s *The Mask of Socrates: The Image of the Intellectual in Antiquity* (Berkeley, 1995) is a brilliant study of how different periods imagined their intellectuals. **Niel R. McLean**'s essay in *Socrates from Antiquity to the Enlightenment* (cited above) introduces Lavater's amazing work on Socrates (see the illustrations on p. 134), and his *The Socratic Corpus* (forthcoming from Cambridge) is eagerly awaited. **Kenneth Lapatin**'s essay 'Picturing Socrates', from the Blackwell *Companion to Socrates,* is a valuable survey.

To follow up on Socratic method (introduced in the text box on pp. 93–4), consult **Gregory Vlastos**, 'The Socratic Elenchus: Method is All' in his *Socratic Studies* (Cambridge, 1994) and **Gary Alan Scott**, editor, *Does Socrates Have a Method? Rethinking the Elenchus in Plato's Dialogues and Beyond* (University Park, PA, 2004). For more on desire, self-control, and the Greeks (as in the text box on pp. 124–5), see **James Davidson**, *Courtesans and Fishcakes: The Consuming Passions of Classical Athens* (London, 1997).

There are fine commentaries on most of the texts in this volume, though they will be most accessible if you know Greek. For Plato's *Apology,* the classic commentary by **John Burnet**, *Plato: Euthyphro, Apology of Socrates, Crito* (Oxford, 1924) has now been supplemented by one by **S. R. Slings and E. de Strycker**, *Plato's Apology* (Leiden, 1994). For the *Gorgias,* see **E. R. Dodds**, *Plato: Gorgias* (Oxford, 1959). I have made liberal use of each of these in preparing this volume.

Glossary

Agora the civic centre of Athens, the equivalent of a forum in the Roman world.

Alcibiades (*c.* 451–403) charismatic and scandalous Athenian leader, and associate of Socrates.

Anaxagoras (*c.* 499–*c.* 428) a **Presocratic** philosopher who may well have been put on trial at Athens for impiety, and whose thought intrigued Socrates early in his career.

Antisthenes (*c.* 446–*c.* 365) a follower of Socrates and author of Socratic works, now lost; he argued that **virtue** was sufficient for the good life, and rejected pleasure.

Anytus (*c.* 443–?) the most prominent figure among the three to speak against Socrates at his trial, the others being **Meletus** and Lycon.

apology a defence speech; both **Plato** and **Xenophon** authored Socratic works with this title.

Aristippus (*c.* 440–?) follower of Socrates and author of Socratic works; he promoted pleasure as the goal of life.

Aristophanes (*c.* 455–386) most prominent comic playwright of his day; author of the *Clouds*, an attack on Socrates.

Aristotle (384–322) student of Plato and the most influential Greek philosopher other than Plato.

Aspasia *de facto* spouse (or, less charitably, mistress) of **Pericles**, called a prostitute by the comic poets but praised by the Socratics.

Assembly the chief governmental body in the Athenian democracy; all adult male citizens were eligible to attend, speak, and vote.

Cicero (106–43) Roman orator, politician, and author.

Council (*Boulē*) a body of 500 Athenian citizens, chosen by lot, that set the agenda for the **Assembly** and provided the committee that presided at its meetings.

Critias (*c.* 460–403) most notorious of the **Thirty Tyrants**, an associate of Socrates and relative of Plato.

daimon a lesser divinity; Socrates claimed to hear from a daimonic sign, a voice somehow related to a daimon.

Delphi site of an oracle of Apollo, the most important oracle in the Greek world.

deme an Athenian's ancestral village or neighbourhood.

Diogenes Laertius (first half of third century AD) biographer of ancient philosophers.

elenchus Socrates' method of interrogating his **interlocutors** and finding contradictions in their beliefs.

epistemology the branch of philosophy devoted to understanding what counts as knowledge.

Gorgias (*c.* 485–380) the most prominent teacher of rhetoric in Socrates' day; title character of a Platonic dialogue.

hedonism the belief that pleasure is the (sole) thing that makes life good.

hoplite a heavily armed Greek infantryman equipped with a spear and large shield.

interlocutor a character engaged in conversation with Socrates.

Meletus (*c.* 430–?) the official prosecutor of Socrates in 399.

mina Greek monetary unit, equal to 100 drachmas, one drachma being a daily wage for a skilled worker in Socrates' day.

nomos (plural, *nomoi*) Greek for tradition, convention, or law; often contrasted with *physis*, nature.

Peloponnesian War (431–404) conflict between Athens and her empire and Sparta and her allies, ending with the defeat of Athens.

Pericles (*c.* 495–429) Athenian statesman, proponent of democracy at home and empire abroad.

physis Greek for 'nature'; often contrasted with *nomos*.

Plato (*c.* 429–347) Socrates' most famous follower, author of philosophical dialogues, most starring Socrates.

Presocratics philosophers active before (and during) Socrates' day; their study centred on the natural world.

Prodicus (second half of the fifth century) a **sophist** who specialized in the study of near synonyms and also authored *Heracles at the Crossroads* (see chapter 4).

satyr or **silenus** a male creature in Greek myth, usually portrayed as a man with certain features of a goat or horse.

Socratic irony Socrates' habit of saying something he doesn't believe, or at least doesn't believe in a straightforward sense.

Socratic paradoxes propositions about morality held by Socrates that seem to contradict common sense. The most famous ones are: (1) no one does wrong (or evil) intentionally; (2) **virtue** consists of knowledge.

Socratic Question, The the attempt to identify the authentic historical Socrates.

sophist an intellectual who travelled from city to city and offered courses in public speaking and other topics for a fee. Among them were Protagoras and **Prodicus.**

sōphrosynē the virtue of moderation or self-control, sometimes extending into self-knowledge (in Plato's *Charmides*, at any rate).

soul (*psychē*) that part of us which gives us life, and is the seat of emotions, of thought, and of the virtues.

stylometry a set of techniques for dating an author's works via small changes in style.

symposium Greek drinking party, the scene of informal philosophizing (at least with Socrates present); title of works by both **Plato** and **Xenophon.**

technē Greek term variously translated as art, expertise, or skill.

Thirty Tyrants the oligarchic regime that ruled Athens from 404 to 403; **Critias** was one of their number.

type A and **type B** scholarly categories for ancient portraits of Socrates; type A versions resemble a **satyr** (or **silenus**) more closely, while type B are more idealized.

virtue (*aretē*) a quality which makes a person (or other thing) a good example of its type.

Xenophon (*c.* 430–*c.* 355) follower of Socrates, and author of the *Memorabilia, Oeconomicus* (*Estate Manager*), *Symposium* and *Apology* (the last two also being titles of works by **Plato**).

Index

Acknowledgements

The author and publishers are grateful for the permissions granted to reproduce images:

Cover image, pp. 26, 143 akg-images/Erich Lessing; p. 9*l* The Art Archive/Archaeological Museum Salonica/Alfredo Dagli Orti; p. 9*c* Portrait bust of Socrates (469–339 BC), copy of Greek early 4th century BC original (marble) (see also 158821), Museo Archeologico Nazionale, Naples, Italy/The Bridgeman Art Library; p. 9*r* Bust of Socrates (470–399 BC) (stone), Greco-Roman/Musei Capitolini, Rome, Italy/Giraudon/The Bridgeman Art Library; p. 13 © The Trustees of the British Museum; p. 15 The Art Archive/Ephesus Museum Turkey/ Alfredo Dagli Orti; p. 18 Ministero per i Beni e le Attività Culturali, Soprintendenza Speciale per i Beni Archeologici di Napoli e Pompei; p. 37 dbimages/Alamy; p. 45 American School of Classical Studies at Athens: Agora Excavations; p. 75 The Art Archive/Ephesus Archaeological Museum, Selcuk, Turkey/Gianni Dagli Orti; p. 82 © The Courtauld Institute of Art, London; p. 86 akg-images/Nimatallah; p. 92 The Art Archive/Staatliche Glypothek Munich/ Alfredo Dagli Orti; p. 95 The Art Archive/ Bodleian Library Oxford; p. 102 Ken Walsh/ Alamy; p. 112 Ken Gillham/Robert Harding; p. 117 Hercules at the Crossroads (oil on canvas), Carracci, Annibale (1560–1609) (Copy)/Gemäldegalerie Alte Meister, Kassel, Germany/© Museumslandschaft Hessen Kassel Ute Brunzel/The Bridgeman Art Library; p. 121 Hercules, or The Effects of Jealousy, c.1498 (engraving), Dürer, Albrecht (1471– 1528) /Private Collection/Photo © Christie's Images/The Bridgeman Art Library; p. 122 bpk/Hermann Buresch; p. 125 Socrates (469–399 BC) visiting Aspasia (colour litho), Daumier, Honoré (1808–79)/Musée de la Ville de Paris, Musée Carnavalet, Paris, France/ Archives Charmet/The Bridgeman Art Library; p. 130 School of Athens, from the Stanza della Segnatura, 1510–11 (fresco), Raphael (Raffaello Sanzio of Urbino) (1483–1520)/ Vatican Museums and Galleries, Vatican City, Italy/Giraudon/The Bridgeman Art Library; p. 134*t* Mary Evans Picture Library; p. 134*b* Mary Evans/Classic Stock/C.P.Cushing; p. 138 The Death of Socrates (470–499 BC) 1762 (oil on canvas) (b/w photo), Saint-Quentin, Jacques Philippe Joseph de (b.1738)/Ecole Nationale Supérieure des Beaux-Arts, Paris, France/Giraudon/The Bridgeman Art Library; p. 148 akg-images.